BUILD THE FORT

...TODAY!

by
Jim Kern

3/21/17

To Laci,
In remembrance
of Jim.

Denise

Illustrated by Debra L. Beverlin

Fourth edition: 2016
Copyright 1989 by Jim Kern
ISBN: 978-0-9622090-4-8

Additional information:
Website: www.jimkern.com
Phone: 210-240-0606 (cell)
Email:
drdenisekern@gvtc.com
jimkern@gvtc.com

Address:
Denise Kern
J.K. Enterprises
100 Winston Place
Spring Branch, TX 78070

Cover art and all illustrations:
Debra L. Beverlin
1207 Union Club Drive
Winter Garden, FL 34787
Layout and Design: Cenveo San Antonio

TABLE OF CONTENTS

Foreword by Dr. John Dumonceaux 5

I. Introduction 7

II. Underlying Beliefs 29
    A. Human Beings are Priceless and Precious
    B. Children are Human Beings, too.
    C. We are All Different
    D. We can Change All Through Our Lives
    E. How We Feel is Important

III. Basic Needs of People 71
    A. The Need for Affection
    B. The Need for Physiological Satisfaction
    C. The Need for Identity
    D. The Need for Safety

IV. Pathways to Pain 117
    A. Pain through Loss
    B. Pain through Choice
    C. Pain through Failure
    D. Pain through Unequal Relationships

V. Pathways to Joy 159
    A. Take Charge of Your Life
    B. Know Your Own Worth
    C. Practice Self Regulation
    D. Learn to Give and Receive
    E. Have fun

VI. In Conclusion 179

FOREWORD
by
Dr. John Dumonceaux
Director of Human Resources
St. Alexius Medical Center
Bismarck, North Dakota

Anyone that has experienced one of Jim Kern's pres-
entations may understand the sense of pride that I felt
when asked to write the foreword to the second edition of
BUILD THE FORT...TODAY! This honor was matched
only by the challenge at hand. I wasn't quite sure how to
take mere words and put them together to adequately
explain the impact that Jim Kern has had on millions of
people in his international travels presenting seminars
and sharing his message of love and hope.

Jim has his roots in education as a teacher and a
coach. I believe Jim is a "master teacher." He believes
the ultimate goal of teaching is to have individuals strive
for continuing self-growth and development. My family
and I have personally experienced this growth through
Jim's message.

Jim's internal sense of power allows him to give to
others a feeling of wholeness. William Shakespeare said
it very well when he said, "They have the power to hurt
and will do none." Jim is very conscious not to misuse
the power he has to touch people. His success is due to a
belief system in which he is a servant to others. He has a
strong desire to help other people. His message of hope
allows people the freedom to seek their own higher
priorities. The people that Jim shares his message with
do grow as persons. They do become healthier, wiser,
freer and because of Jim's message are more likely to
become servants themselves.

I urge you now to relax and to allow the presence of
Jim and his written word to enter your mind and heart. I
urge you to listen to his message and to work with confidence in applying this message of hope and love to your
life.

Introduction

BUILD THE FORT...TODAY!

8

Many times in my work as a teacher of people from elementary school through old age, I have been motivated and influenced by this simple piece of writing presented by Chapman and Counts:

THE MASTER AND THE CHILD
by Chapman and Counts

Greeting his pupils the Master asked: "What would you learn of me?" And the reply came:
HOW SHALL WE CARE FOR OUR BODIES?
HOW SHALL WE REAR OUR CHILDREN?
HOW SHALL WE WORK TOGETHER?
HOW SHALL WE LIVE WITH OUR FELLOWMAN?
HOW SHALL WE PLAY?
FOR WHAT END SHALL WE LIVE?
And the teacher pondered these words in his heart. And his sorrow was great. For his own learning touched not these things.

I've been pleased to have lived during this time with such rapid growth of technology. Mass communication and transportation have emerged as powerful and influential forces. The high tech world of information gathering, storage, and retrieval has dramatically changed the life styles of many people. Often the "high tech" world has over-shadowed what might be called the "high touch" world of our self understanding as well as our personal interactions with others. In the confusion created as new systems grow, people still search for answers to the very basic questions raised in this piece. My purpose in this book has been to share many experiences which have enriched my life and have helped me to find answers to these questions.

As a backdrop for the stories, I have written a brief text which grew directly from several points emphasized in my work as a speaker. These points were chosen as the basis of my work as I studied philosophy under the direction of Dr. Everett D. Lantz at the University of Wyoming. In an article entitled, "What Can We Now Believe?", Dr. Earl Kelley presented twelve points which he suggested form the basis of a belief system he would accept and promote as being worthy of our attention. By synthesizing and combining his twelve tenets, I chose five major principles which best described my life philosophy. I originally presented them as a part of the course requirements. Nine years after that initial presentation, I began my work as a speaker/lecturer and presented those five points throughout the world to audiences with people ranging in age from four years old to ninety plus years.

Many groups have heard me talk of my desire to share ENTHUSIASM and to give ADVICE. These two goals remain important in the presentation of this work. Sharing our enthusiasm with others causes us to lose nothing at all, and we quickly discover that enthusiasm is contagious. Giving advice, on the other hand, can be a perilous adventure.

One major difficulty in giving advice lies in the differences which exist between what one person says and what another person hears. Do you suppose this could really happen?

> She was only five years old, and when she introduced herself, you might have heard her say, "I'm Kathy Anderson, the doctor's daughter," or "I'm the doctor's daughter, Kathy." Each time she mentioned her daddy's occupation. You probably know why she did this—it gave her a bit of a push with her friends.
>
> Her mother, noticing this behavior, took the child aside and said, "Honey, when you introduce yourself in the future, you could say, 'I'm Kathy Anderson.' You could forget that other stuff."

"OK, Mommy," she said.

The very next day in her kindergarten class Kathy had a substitute teacher who didn't know the children, and as she glanced up and down the rows, she noticed one little girl who looked familiar. Could you hear the teacher say, "Aren't you Dr. Anderson's daughter?"

At that, a confused five year old replied, "Well, I always thought I was, but last night Mommy told me I wasn't."

A second and equally distressing difficulty in advising becomes apparent when we realize that when we tell others how to change their behaviors, we might be held to the same standard we have advocated. At some time, each of us has violated the advice we've carefully given others. We could probably take a lesson from this imaginary situation and learn from these imaginary characters:

As the little boy pulled his wagon down the sidewalk, all four wheels fell off and the wagon landed in a heap on the concrete. The boy turned shouting, "Well, I'll be damned!"

He repaired the wagon, continued on his way, and the whole procedure was repeated. Again he made necessary repairs and continued on.

The third time the wagon broke, the child stood right in front of an older clergyman who was appalled at the language of the child and saw an opportunity to deliver an important message to the boy. "I know you're upset when the wheels fall off your wagon, and I know it's better to express your feelings than to press

them down inside you where they can fester and grow.
Don't you think, however, that when you use language
like that out here where anyone could hear you, that
this casts a bad reflection on your home, your school,
and your church? Wouldn't it be better if, when the
wheels fell off your wagon, you
would raise your arms and raise
your eyes and say, 'Hallelujah!!'?"

The child, desiring nothing
more than to be rid of this fellow,
grunted, "All right, I'll do that,"
and he started up the street,
pulling his wagon as before.

The pastor heard the
wagon fall a fourth time,
and turned hoping to
see the results of
his words in
action. The
child
turned, and
began to
say, "Well,
I'll be . . ." He paused and then raised his arms, raised
his eyes and said, "Hallelujah!!"

All four wheels came back up on his wagon, and the
pastor murmured, "Well, I'll be damned."

To complete my short introductory comments, let me
give you some idea about who I am. For twenty years my
life has been dedicated to education, and in that time I
have become convinced that who someone **is** teaches at
least as much as what someone **says**. I believe further
that when students know their teachers and develop
trusting and safe relationships with them, the students
will learn more, learn it more easily, retain it longer, and
apply it more appropriately.

To disclose or not disclose is not the question at all.
When we meet people for the first time we do disclose
ourselves. Verbally and/or non-verbally we tell others
who we are through our dress, our gestures, our expressions and our manner of speaking. In many instances

that first impression we present forms the basis for the relationship and people commonly search for and find evidence in a continuing relationship which supports or contradicts that first impression. The truth of the statement, "You'll only have one chance to make a first impression" deserves careful consideration especially in situations where the interaction will be close and continuous as is the case with teachers of young children.

For the past ten years I've been fortunate to be able to address a variety of groups throughout the world and have enjoyed my first encounters with people a great deal. To be a teacher of many ages of people continues to be one of my goals even now that I've left the formal classroom, and to move toward that goal I repeat again that we often teach as much by what we are as we do in what we say. Many times I've begun with a line similar to this one: "Let me tell you who I am and you'll have a better idea about what our time together might bring." Two incidents from my past clearly demonstrate the importance of disclosure.

A school principal from Green Bay, Wisconsin, provided an early insight into disclosure for me. As I entered the Austen Straubel airport, he greeted me enthusiastically. Though he was happy to have me there with them, he expressed a concern that he wouldn't know how to introduce me to his people. "What can I say about you? You didn't send any information at all."

My rather flippant response was not likely very helpful to him. "Just tell them 'Jim Kern's here and he's on time.'" He snickered nervously and I continued, "You see, I always begin with a bit which I call self-disclosure, and in this time I tell them who I am." He agreed that that would be all right.

We had lunch together and at one thirty the staff was assembled in the meeting room. He walked before them, his hands were shaking and his face extraordinarily white, and he spoke." I'm not going to say much about Jim Kern today because at the beginning of his talk, he does something he calls 'self-disposal'." The crowd laughed heartily, and there we stood.

Years earlier my daughter Carrie had an experience in which she helped me to know how important disclosure is for someone who will be working with little children. Kids often observe well and interpret poorly. Carrie would demonstrate this very clearly.

When she came home after her first day in third grade, Carrie asked, "Dad, do you know who my teacher is this year?" I told her that I didn't know and her tone carried the message as she continued, "It's Mrs. Brown."

"This will not be a good year," I thought.

By the middle of September, we heard Carrie refer to her teacher as "—old Mrs. Brown." By the end of the month we heard "—old fat Mrs. Brown." It's mid-October and the words had changed to "—mean, old, fat Mrs. Brown." When the word "ugly" got into the mix, I thought I must go to school to check it out. I was somewhat embarrassed when my first impression of her teacher led me to believe that Carrie was absolutely right.

Carrie would receive the benefit of her father's 'wise' counsel. "You'll just have to learn to get along with a variety of different people as you go through school and Mrs. Brown will be one of those people." I even suggested that she might come to like Mrs. Brown a good deal if she would just get to know her.

The relationship during the year did not improve.

Then came the last day of the school year. I will never forget Carrie's coming home. She was running so fast that I thought she wouldn't stop for the door. She was shouting at the top of her voice, "Dad,—Dad,—do you know what Mrs. Brown did today?"

"What did she do?"

"Well, Dad, today she wore jeans just like us other kids and she went down the slide."

On this day, the last day of the school year, the kids learned who Mrs. Brown was and they liked her. Mrs. Brown was not old unless we consider forty seven old. Mrs. Brown was not mean and Mrs. Brown was not ugly. Mrs. Brown was fat, but this didn't matter at all to anyone who got to know her as someone who loved kids and wanted most of all for them to learn and to succeed.

My choice of a unique and proper way to disclose myself to you would be to tell you about each of my family members. As you read stories about them, you'll come to know six children and a woman who give my life special meaning. Each one of these seven people brings a special set of gifts which when blended together enhance us all. As you learn about my view of these family members, you will probably learn more about me than about them. I've been convinced over the years that this personal way of presenting myself compliments the information contained on my professional vitae very nicely. Many of you who have worked with me throughout these last ten years on the road will recognize the initial revelations about the kids. For you I've added a short passage to inform you of their current positions in life.

DENISE BEVERLIN KERN, my wife and the CEO of our little business.

Denise was assigned to three small elementary

schools north of Des Moines, Iowa, as a student intern, a part of her counselor education program at Drake University. We were introduced to each other by her supervisor, the elementary counselor who had hired me to speak for two days to student and parent groups in the school. Initially, I was annoyed at the thought that she would be following me around. I assumed that she'd be asking questions and seeking explanations for everything I did with the kids in typical graduate student fashion. Based upon my feelings of annoyance and my assumptions about her behavior, I decided to ignore her as much as possible and concentrate on the work at hand.

I greeted her with that same casual indifference on the second day and once again she was pleasant and businesslike. At the end of the second day, the elementary counselor from the school asked Denise if she'd be willing to take me to the Des Moines airport since she lived nearby. She agreed to do that. We walked together to her car, talked easily, and shared stories about the kids on our trip into and through Des Moines.

We arrived at the departure gate fifty-five minutes before my Braniff flight would leave for Minneapolis. "If my plane is late, we'd have enough time to have dinner," I ventured. "Would you be interested?"

She mentioned having some tentative plans but that she could reschedule them in the event of the possibility that we could have dinner together. I walked alone to the ticket counter and there learned that Braniff had another flight with seats available approximately five hours later. I booked passage on it.

We enjoyed a lovely dinner together.

We were married on the twentieth of July in 1979. She knew at this time that she would have a tremendous amount of responsibility for my four children, two high school students, one college freshman, and one airman stationed at Great Falls, Montana. We moved to Laramie, Wyoming, where she taught on the staff of the University of Wyoming and worked toward her doctor's degree in elementary guidance and counseling.

* * * * * * *

At this time, Doctor Denise Kern (she requests that I call her that whenever others are listening) lives with me near San Antonio, Texas. She volunteers many hours in service to projects for improving the quality of day care for little children. She has just completed her term as the president of Newcomers of San Antonio. She teaches classes in Iowa in the area of reading. She manages all of the details of my traveling and speaking schedule. And in her spare time she makes a home for her family.

CHRISTOPHER JAMES KERN: Born August 20, 1960, in Rochester, Minnesota.

I wanted so badly to have a boy when my first child was about to arrive. I had bet with my brother-in-law that we would have a boy, and I teased relentlessly that he would have blond hair and blue eyes, that he'd be quite bright, and that he'd love football. When Chris finally came, he had blue eyes and blond hair, he was quite bright, and he didn't care at all for football.

He was in tenth grade when I finally coerced him into trying out for the football team. After the first practice he announced for the family to hear, "I just don't like it." After the second practice we heard, "I think it's the stupidest sport ever invented," and after the third practice Chris was very clear, "You know, Dad, it just plain hurts when people slam their bodies into mine like that."

Imposing my will once more on him I said, "Now that you've started, don't quit." His job on the team was to hold the dummy while other people blocked it. Chris was doing his job on the evening before school started. A huge lineman blocked the dummy, and Chris fell back into the ground and broke his arm. He was the happiest kid in southeast Minnesota.

He held his cast high at school the next day and his friends inquired, "How did it happen?"

"It happened in football," he would respond.

"Was it a crushing, head-on tackle that saved the game for the home team?"

"No, I was holding a dummy."

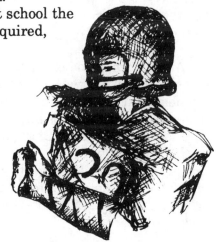

* * * * *

Following his high school graduation, Chris enlisted for four years and served in the United States Air Force. He was stationed for his entire tour in Great Falls, Montana. At this writing Chris lives and works in Laramie, Wyoming, where he is enrolled in a baccalaureate program at the University of Wyoming. Chris skis well and often, plays a respectable game of golf, and may one day graduate from the University, if his father has his way.

CAROLYN ANNE KERN: Born September 22, 1961, in Rochester, Minnesota.

For my second child I ordered a girl who would match my first child. Carrie was born on a Friday evening during football season. She had blond hair and blue eyes, she's quite bright, and she loves football—and many other sports.

As an eight year old Carrie came into our house clad in only her soaking wet bathing suit. She removed it in the bathroom and left it on the carpet in the middle of the bathroom floor. The water which had been in the suit remained hiding in the carpet long after the suit had been moved. I rushed into the bathroom, stockings on, shoes off, and I stepped on one of those cold wet places. The water oozed into my cotton sock. I experienced an immediate rush of anger and I directed my anger toward Carrie.

We worked hard with our children to provide an example for proper ways to handle anger. We had agreed to state specifically what had caused us to be angry and then to tell the kids what course of action we intended to take, thus avoiding the difficulty which might arise when an adult tells a child what must be done, allowing the child to refuse and in refusing, gain much inappropriate power.

I stomped through the house to find this little towhead and as I passed through the living area, I noticed her paper dolls left scattered all about the room. This added to my already crowded storehouse of anger. When I found her, I towered over her and loudly shouted, "When you leave your bathing suit on the bathroom carpet and your paper dolls on the living room floor, I get angry. Now the next time you forget your bathing suit, I'm going to hide it in the Saturday box, and if I find your paper dolls left about, into the wastebasket they go." After a long silent pause, I ended my lecture by saying, "It's as simple as that."

She looked up with those big blue eyes just dancing in her head as

she said, "This week it was my job to clean the dining room. When I started on the table, your files were laid out all over." She pointed and gestured exactly as I had done, and then finished, "So, the next time I find them there, into the wastebasket they go. It's as simple as that!"

* * * * * *

Carrie currently attends the University of Texas at Austin where she will soon earn her master's degree. She took her undergraduate degree at the University of Wyoming in dramatics. For three years, Carrie lived in Washington, D.C. where she sought after her dream to become an actress. She experienced the trials, and the hardships one encounters in a competitive world of the arts. Although her master's degree will be earned in an area much more pragmatically designed to make a living (her father's suggestion), the confidence and abilities she learned through her study of dramatics continue to serve her well.

PAUL WILLIAM KERN: Born November 21, 1962, in Rochester, Minnesota

He'll have brown eyes and brown hair, I predicted and sure enough we received Paul, a big boy exactly as had been ordered. From the earliest days Paul used his charm to get whatever he wanted. He sat in the middle of the living room floor, pointed and grunted, and four people would run to meet his every need. Since everyone served him, Paul apparently decided there was no reason to walk or talk. For eighteen months he sat and directed traffic around him. When we agreed to stop serving him he started to walk and talk immediately.

Potty training time brought some unique problems with this large child, so we taught him to sit backward on the stool, facing the holding tank. He could soon climb up there all by himself, swing his leg across the stool, and the problem was solved.

One Sunday morning, after church, we drove to a very nice restaurant, were seated ahead of the noon rush, and munched on the relish and crackers. Paul announced that he had to go to the bathroom.

"Chris, would you take Paul to the bathroom, please? We'll wait right here for the food." Two little boys strode away filled with confidence.

They were gone for a long time and in their absence the entire restaurant filled with people. Then it happened. Two little boys came running across the room, one of them naked from the waist down. They were both shouting at the tops of their voices, "Dad, Dad, Paul flushed his underpants down the toilet." And, of course, he had done just that. In swinging his leg across the top of the stool, those big boy pants had dropped into the water, the stool was flushed, and they were gone.

* * * * *

Paul traveled for a year with "Up With People" after graduating from Laramie Senior High School. The group traveled through Europe and across the United States spreading the joyous message of love and understanding through music. After his return from the one year tour, Paul lived in Orlando, Florida, where he worked at Rosie O'Grady's place. He moved to San Antonio and worked for the Sea World theme park. He is currently living in Minnesota. At least one of his family members hopes he'll one day return to higher education.

PAMELA LYNN KERN JESKE: Born March 29, 1964, in Rochester, Minnesota

Although we argued about whether Pam was a pretty baby, no one denied that she had a lot of brown hair and big beautiful brown eyes. We watched Pam as she developed into a beautiful child and person.

As the 'baby' of the family, Pam had a chance to learn from her older brothers and sisters, and she was quick to practice whatever she had learned. For example, she knew that when the older children returned home too late, their father would often say, "We did expect you at ten; it's now ten thirty." She probably noticed also that he would then be quiet and give the child a chance to speak.

Pam's opportunity to apply her newly acquired skills came as I prepared to spend three days in western Minnesota. She stood with her back to the kitchen door, her hands on her hips, her eyes cast upward to her father as she said, "Dad, what time will you be home?" I told her that I'd be home Thursday at four thirty and she added, "Have a good trip, I'll expect you then." I drove westward with feelings of warmth knowing that a little girl would be concerned about my returning.

On Thursday I drove back into our small Minnesota town at four fifteen. I could easily have been home by four thirty, but I stopped at my office to open my mail. Time flies when one's having fun. My watch said five forty five as I stopped the car in the driveway and walked into the house.

She exhibited her most severe countenance as she spoke, "Dad. You said you'd be home at four thirty; it's now a quarter to six!" She paused and I began my excuse which she interrupted saying, "No excuses, Dad." She giggled as if to say, "I gotcha!" I held her close.

Two days later I would be leaving for one day and she met me at the door once more. "What time will you be home, Dad?" Five o'clock was my answer and she asked, "Can I trust you this time?"

I left the meeting a little too early, drove a little too fast going home and pulled into the yard as the radio announcer reported the time—three minutes to five. I jumped from the car; I ran to the house; I nearly jerked

the door off the hinges to get in there on time. SHE
WASN'T EVEN THERE!! I felt 'let down.' I wonder if
children feel 'let down' when parents aren't there to
notice their successes.

* * * * *

Pam is married and has two beautiful little children
at this point in her life, my first two grandchildren.
Andrew, age three, and Sara, age one, live with their
mother in Minnesota. Pam devotes full time to raising
Andrew and Sara and finds her cup overflowing with the
affection she receives as she attends to and loves them.
Pam has completed much of her training program toward licensure to be a beautician and hopes to work on
her college degree as that becomes possible.

KATHRYN RACHEL MARIE KERN: Born November 18, 1983, in Laramie, Wyoming.

The events surrounding Katie's appearance nearly
five years ago in 1983 remain clear in my mind. We were
pleased when Denise became pregnant with Katie,
although the pain of an earlier miscarriage was ever
present. I was working with a large group of junior high
school students when the urgent message came that I
would have to go home for an "emergency". A long plane
ride and a long drive from Denver to Laramie preceded a
long labor period. I tried to remain alert and helpful, but
the fatigue proved too much and I fell asleep leaving all
the work of delivering this child to Denise and Anita, her
close friend who had served as her coach through the
LaMaze' experience. Katie chose to come into the world
face up and this made her delivery just a bit more difficult than it would have needed to be. (I have since speculated that she chose this method of arrival so she
wouldn't miss anything. She still misses very little).

Our preparations for Christmas of 1987 were finished
well in advance of Christmas Eve day and my well
organized wife had placed the gifts 'from Santa' in our

bedroom closet on a shelf well out of reach of our four year old, Katie, and our two year old, Jamie. Somehow, Katie sensed that there must be something special in that closet as she seized every opportunity to push close to Mom or Dad as they chose clothing and brought it forth from that dark area.

On one of those trips into the closet, the sharp eyes of a four year old spied a special package about six feet above the floor and when Mom was upstairs and Dad was in the living room, the temptation became too great. She climbed the shelves to complete her investigation. I had heard the noises and couldn't have missed the guilt written all over that mischievous grinning face as Katie joined me in the living room.

"Katie, have you seen something which you shouldn't have seen?" Her weight shifted from foot to foot and her fingers found their way into her mouth. In a tone which fathers learn to use when they want to be unmistakably and forcefully confrontational while giving the child a chance to confess without inviting further wrath, I spoke to her, "Katie - - -

25

what have you done?"

She recalled a line which she had undoubtedly heard many times, "I want to think about that for a little while."

* * * * * *

Katie has completed her second pre-school experience. For most of one year Kate attended two days a week of the St. Mark's school in San Antonio, and she wrapped up a complete year of work in the Acorn School attending four afternoons per week. She continues to demonstrate her ability to climb and appears to be well on her way to establishing herself as an athletic person.

JAMES TROY KERN: Born June 14, 1985, in Laramie, Wyoming.

Throughout her pregnancy with Jamie, Denise believed that there might well be two babies instead of the one we had anticipated. He came much more easily than his sister and he came with big dimples, big hands and big feet. He was prized by all of us including his big sister, Katie. Then, we prepared to bring him home from the hospital, and Kate made it very clear that Jamie should stay in the hospital.

When Jamie decides to grow from stage to stage, his change happens instantly. One evening at dinner, Jamie made it very clear that he was not going to sit in his high chair. We put him in a booster and he became a different person. Denise and I left for a two week trip abroad and left our relatively silent son with grandparents. We returned to find a little boy who would not stop talking. His potty training, his sleeping in a big bed, learning new skills, and his leaving Mom and Dad have all followed this pattern.

Each time we launch the boat, start the engine, and head out to the lake, I have taken off my hairpiece and placed it in a secure place. I was not aware of having said during this process, "I'd better put my hair away so the wind doesn't blow it off."

Jamie, at two years and ten months, had just spent several days away from his daddy and now on my first day home he is being particularly helpful. He'd brought me a newspaper, he'd helped me get my shoes on, and finally he approached carrying my hairpiece in both hands.

"Daddy," he said so seriously, "maybe I can wear one of these hairs when the wind blows all my hair off."

* * * * * *

Jamie has begun his pre-school experience this year at the Acorn school. **Everyone** was ready.

Part I

Underlying Beliefs

BUILD THE FORT...TODAY!

You've learned about my family and their importance in my life. The next level of disclosure lies in the
area of my philosophy. My purpose in this section will be
to share five beliefs which I have used as the principal
guides for my behavior. In the previous section I told you
of the work by Dr. Earl Kelley from which I've extracted
the basis of my belief system. Dr. Kelley wrote primarily
for the education community, but these principles are
easily applied to all areas of life and work, especially if
we are to believe in their precious nature . I have strived
to place these principles at the basis of my life and my
work. I submit them to you in this book with the hope
that you might find something you can use in your life.

I've not arranged these statements in order of their
importance to me as each would hold approximately
equal value, but rather have just ordered them to allow
for easy discussion.

I'm very much aware that accepting these principles
and applying them are two very separate tasks. Many
times when I've failed to live in accordance with my beliefs, I review my behavior to attempt to grow more
consistent and more congruent. I'm committed to move
toward that ideal wherein my thoughts, my words, and
my actions will find their roots in these general statements.

I'm convinced that the simplest presentation of our
thoughts yields the most complete understanding. By
using stories and simple language some of the greatest
teachers in history taught the masses valuable lessons
and insights. When I read, "Do Unto Others As You
Would Have Them Do Unto You," I question my having
chosen five points. However, I have chosen five and now

I intend to present these beliefs in a simple straightforward style, a conversational style, if you please.

Bo Lozoff, writing for a prison project, presents a thought I'd choose for a preface to my sharing of my beliefs with you:

> "There is no spiritual practice more profound, no lifestyle more creative or productive than being kind to one's family, neighbors, the cashier at the grocery store, the unexpected visitor, the person who does the laundry or picks up the garbage, or any other of the usually 'invisible' people whose paths we cross in the course of any normal day of our lives."

Principle #1

HUMAN BEINGS ARE PRICELESS AND PRECIOUS.

I believe that people are much more important than things, and I've watched as many folks raised their hands in agreement. Still, so many times our words and our actions suggest just the opposite of this belief. How many of us can recall specific instances when things appeared to be more important? Consider the little child who spills food or drops and breaks something in our homes (often something which had little value before it was broken).

Put yourself in the place of someone involved in an accident. Do you remember the time you had just a little accident with the family car? Was the experience more traumatic if the car was 'brand new'? To separate someone's behavior from the person allows us to regard people as priceless and precious despite the damage to the car.

> How many of you have put a dent or a scratch on the family car? How many of you can remember what some significant other said when you brought the car home to explain what had happened? Was the magni-

tude of the response correlated in any way with the relative newness of the car?

We were more than a thousand miles from home when the phone rang and I answered. My son Chris's voice from that great distance away came clearly, though hesitantly, across the miles, "Guess what, Dad." These words frequently cause parents to sit down. I sat down.

"Chris, I won't guess because whatever I guess will be worse than what's happened. What is it?"

"Well, Dad," he began slowly, "as I was cruising to work this morning (long pause) at five miles per hour, (longer pause) I cruised into the side of a Midland Co-op oil truck."

Then, with my son in trouble those many miles away, I asked, "How's your car?" He was prepared for that response. He reminded me of what I've said in my lectures for many years, that people are more important than things.

He had made a mistake. Driving northward very slowly, he looked to the west, out the side window, to see the results of an accident in the ditch. A moment of inattention while his vehicle continued to move, albeit slowly, resulted in a crash. I'm aware now that asking about his welfare first would have been more in keeping with my belief.

Start with yourself. Each person has gifts just waiting to be loved out of him or her, yet some of us become our own judge, jury, and executioner. Many of us deny or hide our talents and run the risk that we will forget we have them. Instead, you might ask yourself: "What do I like about myself?" or "What would others appreciate in me as they get to know me better?"

Secondly, consider the priceless, precious nature of the people in your family. Sometimes, we assume that those nearest us "know" that we value and cherish them, therefore, we do not need to express our appreciation. Can you imagine the change that will appear in our children when we begin to pay attention to all of their positive experiences, to their victories and successes? Can you dream of what might happen if we'd treat our wives and our husbands with extra love and respect all of the time? Wouldn't we improve our closest relationships if we would treat family members with at least the same respect we offer the clerk in a grocery store? Use a family member's name when you're not angry, touch another in a special way, express your appreciation and the world changes.

A school superintendent in southern Iowa reported that he touched his wife just before they went to sleep, he used her name just as he'd been instructed in the workshop that day, and he told her he loved her. The next morning she revealed that she'd not slept a wink wondering what he had done wrong.

Thirdly, imagine what our neighborhoods would be like if we loved our neighbors as ourselves. (Some have reported that we DO and therein lies our problem!) My neighbors over the years have been wonderful people. Several years ago, I'd asked Merle, my neighbor just to the north of my home in Wyoming, to watch over my place while I was away for the winter. I returned to the cabin unexpectedly in the fall, entered to get the motorcycles out, and he walked up "- - - just checking to see who was here."

Another of my Wyoming neighbors tells stories and entertains people every chance he gets. Not only is Troy a priceless, precious human being, he's also a superb helper.

Troy has become the kind of friend who seems to appear whenever I need help. Chris, age 10, and I had been nailing down roof boards since early this morning. We worked our way toward the peak of the roof on this

34

cold but clear and quite pleasant December day. We
had enough boards to finish the job, but all too soon the
sun would disappear behind those western mountain
peaks and in less than one hour the temperature would
plunge quickly to intolerably low levels. I knew that
two hours would give us ample time to reach the peak.
Closing the roof over the building to the harsh weather
would protect tools and materials inside and would
allow us to work on those days in winter when outside
work is unthinkable.

"How're you doing?" he asked as he stepped onto
the roof from the ladder. He was wearing his nailing
apron and carrying his hammer.

Together we three nailed and fitted and cut those
boards. The work became easier and his comments and
stories caused us all to chuckle. He taught Chris a way
to prevent cold fingers from being whacked by the
hammer head. "Just keep both hands on the handle,"
he advised, "and you'll never hit your fingers."

One hour fifteen minutes later we climbed down
the ladder, went inside to survey the day's work, and

enjoyed the beauty of a Wyoming sunset together. The
temperature outside at sundown dropped to eleven
degrees below zero.

Principle # 2

KIDS ARE PEOPLE, TOO.

"Raise your hand if you believe that children are priceless and precious human beings. Do we really believe that children are more important than things?" People raise their hands, some hesitantly, and I tease them by asking if they're truly convinced. Our children are **our most valuable national resource**, more important than our economic development, more important than technology, more important than agriculture and more important than oil. Today's children will soon grow to become decision makers and caretakers of all these other things as we move aside and entrust our world to them.

Nearly all people realize the obvious truth in the statement that children are people, and yet, in practice we sometimes forget that children have thoughts, feelings, desires, and dreams all their own. They come through us into the world as totally dependent tiny creations, and upon their arrival people often express thoughts like these:

"What a beautiful baby!"

"Look at those pretty eyes. Just like his dad's."

"She seems to be so alert—so intelligent."

"It's a miracle. Look at him!"

He's such a good little boy!"

Loving friends and relatives want to hold the baby, and they compete for that honor. It's not uncommon for people to take far too many pictures of the baby, especially when the baby is the first child in a family. The child hears the message from every quarter, "You're a precious priceless person."

In five short years, this cherished baby has made many changes and the responses from significant others have also changed. Do you have a five year old in your life? Have you experienced the company of this person on a trip through a modern super market? No? Have you given any thought to the inevitable circumstances of such a trip ?

To shop in a modern supermarket with a five year old boy helps parents to see how much our responses to our babies have changed. Grocers seem to put everything a child might want on the bottom shelf where the child can see it, marshmallows, chocolate chips, Cracker Jack, and now Jello. (Thanks to Bill Cosby and television, every three year old can read 'Jello') This placement of items only contributes to the potential conflict which will arise. To help parents through a potentially traumatic experience, carts were invented.

Perhaps the inventor reasoned this way: "As mothers move through the store picking up groceries, the child could push the cart."

The plan works fine in our minds, but in the store we discover quite a different reality. Mom takes ten steps down the aisle, the cart crashes right up the back of her legs, and she turns to speak to her child. Recall now the comments Mom made about her baby at the time of its birth. Would she be consistent if she would now say, "That's OK, Honey, you're a human being."

Children often hear something closer to this, "You idiot!" At this point Mother pushes the cart and the child acts like the idiot as HE digs through the groceries.

If parents believe they've won the battle in the store, just wait until they arrive at the checkout counter. There in many stores they'll be confronted with two or more shelves of candy and gum.

The child desperately wants something, the mother is exhausted, and the clerk wants to make matters better so she hands the child one stick of gum.

"And what do you say?" Mother demands. The boy pauses, looks up innocently, and says, "Charge it!"

All too soon our children begin the process of leaving their parents. They leave home to begin school, and elementary teachers assume an important responsibility, our children's education. Very often the relationship between the child and the teacher can enhance the experiences of the years spent with mother and dad. On some occasions the things that happen in the school can destroy the previous five or six years experience.

Since our teachers will become very influential in shaping the lives of today's young people, they deserve a good bit of help and support from our entire society. Understanding our children and effectively communication with them will be much easier if parents and teachers hold similar beliefs about kids and how they grow. All adults in the lives of children must be reminded to

see the world as a child sees it and to begin at an appropriate level for the child in this teaching/learning process. To do this more easily and efficiently we might want
to keep the child part of us alive...forever.

I have asked in many sessions, "What is a child?" A
wide range of answers will follow. Then, I ask the people
if they know of some folks who have let the child part of
them die. Some will suggest that they know many, even
in young adulthood, who have lost track of that most
important part of themselves. Still others tell of people
well up in years who have a very active and alive child
part—too alive and all too visible, sometimes.

Do you stop being a child when you reach a certain
age? Is it age 15? 18? 21? Or is being a child more a
function of attitude than a function of years?

A small congregation extended an invitation for me
to speak on the importance of families and children
during the Sunday worship service on a beautiful
autumn morning in Lone Rock, Wisconsin. The service
seemed expecially inspiring. The people were enthusiastic. I took the microphone in my hand after a warm
introduction and walked close to the people to chat
about families and their importance to early development of our children. To promote discussion, I raised
rhetorically the question we're considering here, "What
is a child?" After quite a long pause, I stated my belief,
"A child is a human being who has not yet reached his
or her ninety-fourth birthday."

Upon hearing those words, a woman in the congregation stood and said, "I've got one more year being a
child!"

She was ninety-three years old. The smile on her
face and the sparkle in her eye left little doubt that the
child in her was very much alive. Margaret was a very
impressive woman who knew the value of laughing, of
crying, of being afraid and expressing anger. She kept
the child part of herself alive in many ways.

When she was ninety-six her friends came to her to
explain that they couldn't let her live alone in her upstairs apartment any longer. They told her that the
whole process was too hard for them and that things

were very difficult for her
as well. They had decided to
move her into a rest home
where she would share a
suite with her two older
sisters—one was ninety-
nine and one was one
hundred one!

Several months later
the oldest of the three gals
died. I went to be with
Margaret, took her hands in
mine and expressed my
concern for her at this time
of·her sorrow, "I'm so sorry
about your sister."

Without a moment's
pause, Margaret said, "Oh,
she died, and we're kinda
glad—we needed the
space." The child in this dear person will never die.

Only a few months later word came that Margaret
had passed away. A thoughtful friend sent along her
obituary which was so simple and straightforward, I'd
guess that Margaret wrote it herself. The very short
piece ended by telling the world that she had died "...at
age ninety-seven after a short illness in the rest home."

The spirit of that beautiful child goes with me
wherever I go now. Whenever I'm tempted to take
myself a bit too seriously, I shut my eyes, her face and
smile reappear and she seems to say again as she did
so often, "Jim, it's OK to be afraid, it's OK to be angry,
it's OK to to cry, and it's OK to laugh." I hear these
thoughts again and again, to remind me that it's
important for us all to let our child part live...forever.

We've agreed that children (anyone of us under
ninety four years old, remember) are important. Now a
further consideration: "Just how important are they?"
My favorite response to this question was offered by a
ninety one year old retired pastor I met at a senior
center in Wisconsin. After I had posed the question to
the group, he stood up, leaned on his cane, and stated his

belief with the authority of many years experience with children behind him, "They're all we've got." I agreed with him. Indeed, our children are all that we have.

Suppose a visitor from another world were to appear and demand that all people would have to make a choice, each of us must give up all that we own or one child. Which would it be for you?

Some might choose to give up a child. Many who wouldn't think of doing that may say things to our children or do things to our children which would indicate that we believed just the opposite. Many children face the hurts of embarrassment, abandonment, humiliation, physical abuse, and neglect every day of their lives. Many well-intentioned parents say words which can hit a child as hard as any fist, and occasionally the hurt of words lasts much longer. I respect very much the speaker who suggested that our kids 'hear' what we say about them even if they're not present. When we believe kids are this important, our responses to them change.

In junior and senior high school assemblies, I meet some of my favorite 'children.' (When I use this word with them, I want them to know the meaning this word carries for me.) After working through my introduction and my view of the importance of all people, I ask these young people to raise their hands if they believe that kids are people, too. Sounds of unanimous and enthusiastic agreement fill the auditorium as they raise their hands high.

"How many of you have younger brothers and sisters?" Again many hands go into the air. "Are they human beings?" I ask, raising my hand as a model for their behavior. Few raise their hands and several even laugh as they call out, "No!!"

I spar with them a bit about **having** younger siblings as well as **being** younger siblings. I comment briefly, and often lightly, about the problems of using violence to settle differences. The mood in the auditorium begins to change from light and meaningful to much more serious, as I ask them to recall a time when adults want children to listen, to pay attention. "Do any of you remember what your parents or teachers said to you when they believed you weren't paying attention?"

Many youngsters recall not only the words, but also the tone of voice and volume of parents, teachers, and other adults in their lives. " How many of you have heard one of these questions: 1) Why don't you listen when I talk? or 2) Why can't you pay attention to me? or 3) How many times do I have to tell you? or 4) Are you deaf, for goodness sakes?"

Later when the young person needs an adult to listen to the sharing of a hurt, a fear, or a joyous experience, kids hear us say quite different things. Kids talk very openly about having heard all six of these replies. Do any of them sound familiar to you?

"Not tonight!"

"Later!"

"I'm too tired!"

"I'm too busy!"

"Some other time!" or

"Just a minute!" (a 'minute' kids know has more than sixty seconds).

The seven year old boy asked his father, "Daddy, could you build me a fort?", and Daddy said that he could. The child's every waking moment was filled with the excitement and anticipation of working on his own fort.

The child was nearly bursting with enthusiasm as his father came home from work the next day. "Tonight, Daddy, can we build the fort?"

"Not tonight, son, I'm just too tired."

On the second night daddy postponed once more saying, "Tonight I have a report to do. I must be finished by tomorrow."

On the third night Daddy's explanation was a bit longer, "Son, your mother and I have made a promise to go to a party. Do you understand about promises?"

Indeed, the child did understand about promises.

These were followed with other statements to postpone the building, still the child persisted.

On a Friday morning, the child heard his daddy say, "Tonight you hurry right home from school and we'll build your fort." The excitement of a child is indescribable. Not one thing will be gained from today's experience in school as a child thinks only of that moment when he will work with his dad on that special fort.

The bell rang signalling the end of the day. The boy leaped from his desk, bolted out the front door, and maybe he reasoned like this: "I can run all the way home; it's only seven blocks."

With a head full of dreams and happiness, the boy ran as fast as he could, not at all aware of the too familiar world passing by. As he entered the busy road, he looked neither left nor right. The truck appeared out of nowhere and the small body was hit. The ambulance took the lad to the hospital emergency room where the first evaluation contained only one word, "Coma!"

Dad received the call and he drove recklessly to the hospital, pushed past people to enter his son's room and stood for what must have seemed an eternity at the foot of his child's bed. Father watched as two little eyes opened, a little smile appeared, and a voice just a bit too weak uttered the boy's last words, "Daddy, we won't have to build that fort tonight after all."

The child died.

I believe that the child is OK, but Dad is not OK. Dad is thinner now, and he's quieter now. Dad loses his hair in circular patches and when it grows back, it grows back without color. He very likely wonders where to turn for relief from the guilt and the pain. To whom can he say, "I wish I had never postponed those requests"? We may lose daddy, too.

We can learn from the experiences of others. I have decided that I will never again say to a child one of those delaying responses. Instead I'll be saying, "How long do you think it will take?" When the child says, "Three minutes," or "Five minutes," or "Seven minutes," I'll realize I have as many minutes as the child has requested. What could be more important than spending time with our most valuable resource, our children?

The hospital staff had heard this story as a part of the morning presentation. Later, when one of the hospital administrators returned to the afternoon session, he shared this personal experience. During the lunch hour, his son had asked him if they might take a bike ride together. Dad recalled how many times he had delayed the request. Today he said, "How long do you think it will take?" and an excited young boy shouted, "Just once around the block!!"

FOR YOU DADS: Would you consider this? The next time your child asks for your time or attention, please do these three things: 1) put your newspaper down, 2) turn your television set off, and 3) use your child's name as you ask, "How long do you think it will take?" When you do these things, Dad, you make a large investment in the future of your child. You could very well be saving your child's life and you will help in the creation of a better world for us all.

FOR YOU MOMS: Would you consider this? When a child asks for your time, would you please: 1) put your newspaper down, 2) turn your television set off, and 3) ask the child how long this will take. And, Moms, doesn't it seem that we always ask more of you? Don't you get tired of it all? Mothers, would you let the cleaning wait? Many of you are aware that despite advances in the sharing of parental responsibilities, you are often left with the cleaning. You all know that cleaning can wait, kids can't wait.

FOR ALL WHO LOVE KIDS: When we who love the children stop listening to them or giving them attention, someone else listens and that someone else takes our children away from us.

Principle # 3

WE'RE ALL DIFFERENT.

Each of us is different from the rest of us in our physical characteristics. We differ even more in our non-physical make-up, and in combinations of body and soul we are each one a unique creation.

Being different does not make one better than nor worse than another. In some ways each of us is gifted, each of us is handicapped, and each of us is limited. Frequently people have received and internalized information which causes them to believe that they are inadequate, inferior to, or less than other people. Having accepted this 'reality' as truth, those people live out the judgments and the world loses the special gifts within these folks. At times people adopt a false view of themselves, believing and acting as if they are considerably superior to all others. I believe this view will adversely affect all of their relationships.

One of the consequences of being different is the very common use of labels to identify those who are different. Many tools can be used to create a better world or misused to create pain, destruction, and despair. Labels have that power. Having identified and labeled conditions of illness or deficiency, people in the helping professions can deliver proper assistance, medication, or rehabilitation. This represents a use of labels. Labels misused can deliver tremendous isolation or hurt, and they may serve as self fulfilling prophecies. The misuse of a label might destroy in the labelled person any positive view of self.

As children many of us heard these common labels: fat, skinny, short, tall, stupid, smart, rich, poor, cry baby, sickly, and the list goes on. Many of us could accept ourselves knowing that, while the label was partly true though a bit hurtful, we could focus on other traits which brought us balance. When I was growing up,

I heard many labels and learned from my mother to
recite these words, "Sticks and stones may break my
bones, but names will never hurt me." Even as I said or
thought those words, I felt the hurt of the names and the
taunting. I withdrew from my peers. I turned to my
mother for help and received protection and pity. There
were times when these caused even more hurt. The
protection, especially, distanced me even further from
potential friends.

The words which hit closest to differences perceived
as weaknesses may do the greatest damage. Someone
with a birth defect or deformity may hide the deficiency
to protect the bearer from further ridicule and hurt.

When she was born, her left arm was just like ours;
her right arm ended at her elbow. When she received
her first prosthesis, a small hook-like device, she was
able to carry things and to participate in activities with
the other children in her neighborhood. Throughout
her early years she lived a life much like any other
child. She had her moments of joy and sorrow, her ups
and downs.

When she left home to begin her kindergarten
experience at age five, she had the normal fears of a
child starting school, but she was very excited to begin.
During recess of that first day, a classmate from
overtown shouted out these hurtful words, "Captain
Hook goes to our school."

Seeing this as very funny, many join what will
become a chant and day after day a little girl finds less
joy in her school experience. Protective and comforting
words from the teacher may drive the teasing under-
ground for a time. Apart from the teacher, she heard
the words, saw the taunting and ridiculing looks, and
felt the hurt of isolation from her classmates.

Her second prosthesis was in place as she entered
first grade remembering the fear and loneliness of last
year. Her mother had assured her that this year would
be different because the hook was replaced with her
new stainless steel pincher. The same little boy who
had started the taunts last year shouted, "Captain
Hook has a new arm." Hurts are magnified when you're

six. She believed the whole world contributed to a hurtful conspiracy.

The teasing lasted along with the prosthesis throughout the elementary school years. Many teachers sought ways to stop the teasing but were unsuccessful. By the end of sixth grade, she had become a lonely young woman finding much comfort in activities she could accomplish alone.

Young people experience important changes during the junior high school years, changes which are magnified through the hurt of ridicule and isolation. She did not enjoy these years at all.

One of her tenth grade teachers invited her to share with her classmates the experience of living with a prosthesis. She was nervous as she stood before her tenth grade classmates. She held the first of her prostheses so all could see it and explained the feelings she recalled. She went into much detail about wearing the hook, continued by demonstrating the mechanics of her pincher, and concluded by telling of a new prosthesis she'd received which looks very much like the human arm. Her sharing included some humor and provided for her a new acceptance amongst her peers.

She married right after high school graduation, and moved away from her home area. When her first child was expected, she wrote saying that she prayed during her pregnancy that her child would be healthy and that the child would have two arms.

At times statements made by responsible and well-intentioned people deliver hurts similar to the hurts created by childhood taunting. Imagine the thoughts which run through the mind of a custodian dressed in his work uniform who hears a mother tell her child to be sure to work hard in school and go to college so "—you don't end up like that man."

Occasionally people in very influential positions reveal their deep seated insensitivities as they go about their normal work day.

After two aborted landing attempts in the snow-blown north country in February, our plane bumped down onto the asphalt runway. As we coasted to a stop I thought to myself "—I haven't charged this group enough." (I amuse myself like this whenever I'm risking life and limb.) I rented a car and drove the entire eighty miles in blizzard conditions on black ice. I worried about my safety in this harsh climate, and at the end of the trip I was exhausted.

Waiting just inside the school door the next morning, the principal recognized me walking toward him and spoke in a very impersonal way. Quite early in the conversation he shared this thought, "You're so damned expensive." (Again I wondered if I had charged this group enough.) Surely he was only teasing. I asked for clarification. He responded to my request without smiling or giving any non-verbal cue that he was not serious. "It means we're going to do only one school assembly." This confused me even more.

I explained that I would be available through the entire morning and that I would prefer to be busy than to be sitting around with nothing to do. My plan for this day would be to work with kids in the morning, teachers in the afternoon, and a parent group in the evening. Kids can be excellent recruiters of parents, but only if they have time to be committed to the value of the program. "So," I offered, "we can do as many student meetings as you'd like. I'll be here all day."

He left no doubt about who would be in charge. "We're going to do one!"

I stood nervously inside the cold gymnasium door beside this stern-faced principal to watch the kids come in for the assembly program. They were too orderly and too quiet, 'afraid' I thought. They ranged in age from seniors in high school seated at the top of the bleachers to the third graders seated in the front row. I thought to myself that this would be impossible as I surveyed somber faces of about 150-175 young people. My discussion of dating and drug abuse will certainly be appropriate for the older ones, but what of the third graders? I remembered previous experiences with third graders who, when asked to raise questions during a similar meeting, spoke in typical third grade tone and manner, "Do you have any pets?" I shared that I had a black labrador dog. The second question, "What color is it?"

I wondered nearly aloud about the interest level and patience level of sophomores, juniors, and seniors during similar exchanges.

We were almost ready to begin when a very young teacher walked up to the right of the principal and asked, "Could I bring my class, too?"

"No," he boomed. "They won't understand a word he says." The third graders will need to understand. Who could possibly not understand what I'll be saying? I was really puzzled.

"Please," she pleaded, "we'll sit right here in this empty space, and we'll be quiet."

"All right, but if they make one sound, this will be the last program they'll ever attend." I'm quite sure he had not delivered this threat to the kids already seated, but this would be the condition for the thirteen junior and senior high school special education kids she ushered into the gym and onto the bleachers. She and another woman sat amongst these different youngsters and I believed we'd now be ready to begin.

When he lifted the microphone off the lectern, he appeared to be ready to introduce me. Instead he scolded all present for making noise as they climbed onto those wooden bleachers. (Don't they always make noise when someone walks on them?) He called my name and admonished them to "—pay attention and listen carefully to whatever he says." I couldn't believe my ears, and I wondered if they would dare to laugh with me.

The kids were magnificent. The juniors and seniors were patient as the third graders asked their ques-

tions. The third graders seemed more than a bit
interested as I talked of dating and drugs to the older
ones.

I placed the microphone down at the end of the
presentation. I was aware of the polite applause offered
up by the student body. As I walked toward the gymnasium doors, I noticed Paul arise from the special group
to walk toward me. Paul was a Down syndrome child
about seventeen. He placed both arms about my mid-
section and squeezed so hard that air left my body. I
placed my head directly down on the top of his head
and in doing that I could see the students. Almost
immediately the enthusiasm of the applause picked up.
Do kids foresee miracles before adults do?

I was finished hugging Paul so I gave him that
little non-verbal signal which means, "I'm done hugging you now." But Paul wasn't finished; he squeezed
me tightly and I realized I'd not be able to walk away
with a body clinging to mine, so I squeezed back and
looked once more toward the students. I swear some of
them were getting tears in their eyes.

Paul released me and I watched as he walked away
in the opposite direction from which he had come.
Though I was bewildered I supposed he knew what he
was doing, so I turned to continue my trip to the door. I
nearly collided with Charles, a cerebral palsied lad. He

hugged me for only a moment before he followed Paul. Then came Emily followed by ten other special kids, each one bringing a warm embrace to exchange for one from me.

The students stood to applaud as the special kids led by Paul returned to their seats. I walked to a spot right beside the principal. I really felt smug. He turned to speak to the special education teacher and as he spoke I felt quite a range of emotions.

"I was wrong," he began. Could it be that he IS sensitive to kid's needs after all? He continued, "I still don't think they understood what he said,—." No, I thought, it was just a momentary slip-up; he's still talking like the insensitive autocrat I'd imagined him to be. Then, he concluded his thought, "—but they seemed to know that he cared for them."

My heart leaped in my breast and an old lesson was stirred to a higher level of awareness: "KIDS DON'T CARE WHAT YOU KNOW UNTIL THEY KNOW THAT YOU CARE."

The child with her prosthetic arm, the special kids, and many people born to be different have so much to offer. One such person came into my life just prior to an inservice workshop held in the fall at Derby, Kansas. He sat to my right and offered his hand to receive mine as we exchanged first names. His hand had only one finger, and his other hand was badly deformed. "Born that way," he explained. "Only one baby in a million has this problem."

"Was it hard in school?"

"Only when they called me a one fingered baboon, but I took care of that pretty quickly."

He had no idea who sat beside him and listened to his grumbling about "—these meetings" being a waste of time, and that he was "—forced to attend." He thought he could use the time better getting his room ready.

I was introduced to speak and he put his head down in embarrassment. At the end of my presentation he brought to me a collage which he had produced during my talk depicting each point of my speech. He gave it to me, perhaps as an apology for the feelings he had expressed.

The drawing demonstrated a marvelous sensitivity and insight into the feelings of people—and clearly expressed with pictures the five major beliefs of the presentation I'd just completed. I've come to respect Mr. Richard Dolloff, Jr. very much—he's "One-in-a-Million."

And, let me present one more special person. He came into my life initially as I watched him on television.

"That's Incredible" brought this person into my living room and I doubted the honesty of the presentation as it continued. We were told that he was born with no eyes, that he didn't hear, that his fingers were badly deformed, and that his feet were severely turned inward. We were told how the boy was taken home by a retired nanny past sixty years old. The woman would care for him and love him for the rest of his life which many believed would be very short, maybe five years. She gave him extraordinary care, providing movement and exposure to music and a strong religious faith. People reported that she dragged him about from time to time on a sheet tied about her waist.

For eighteen years she cared for this most different child. One night after she'd put him to bed and as she was resting in her bedroom, she heard the sound of music from the piano room. She hurried to the room, turned on the light, and beheld the boy sitting on the bench and playing the piano. He played classical music and popular music and hymns. She didn't know whether to call a priest or the police. The story appeared first on local television and then on "That's Incredible."

Watching the program I wondered about the truth of the story and dismissed it all shortly as another attempt to sensationalize the otherwise bland programming contained on commercial television. It's just another trick, I thought.

Years later the Green Bay, Wisconsin, foster parent group provided me an opportunity to address their people. As I prepared for my two hour morning presentation, a lady came forward filled with enthusiasm telling me that Leslie would probably come to play at noon. "Leslie?" I wondered; "Who's this Leslie?"

The morning session was finished, and lunch was about to be served. He walked into the room with his hands on his foster father's shoulders, shuffling his feet along and making unintelligible sounds as the older man and woman moved with him toward the piano. I helped prepare the bench for him and the moment he sat down, he began to play. His performance was just incredible. He played easily with both hands and occasionally picked up the melody with his left hand. He sang the songs in more than one language. A woman from the crowd was asked to play. Upon completion of her song, he sat down and repeated it exactly as she had played it.

While he played, his foster mother, well up in years, ran around the room. She sang the songs wonderfully out of tune. As she rounded the corner and started toward our table, she threw her skirt into the air and frolicked much as a very young person would do. She sprinted toward our table. Just before she arrived she went down to her stomach, slid under the table, and came out on the other side. Someone at my

table said, "If she were my mother, I wouldn't travel
with her."

As we snickered we were very much aware that her
gift of love to this different human being was magnificent and we discussed her accomplishment, an unpar-
alleled commitment to his development.

Principle # 4

WE CAN CHANGE AND CHANGE FOR THE BETTER FOR AS LONG AS WE LIVE.

To grow is to change. People tend to become comfortable with their lives and they "kick back," stop moving
into new areas, stop risking and stop growing. Life
begins to look boring to these people; self destructive
behaviors become an integral part of these lives; and
despair moves in to replace the excitement of continuing
growth.

Some suggest that changing stops when we reach a
certain age. After that age people use excuses like "—you
can't teach an old dog new tricks," and other avoidance
techniques to explain their stagnation. I believe we can
continue to change forever and that it's never too late to
attempt something new and different. The joy, the
excitement, and sometimes the embarrassments people
encounter as they risk and change can be contagious.
The success stories of people changing the direction of
their lives after they're up in years abound. We'd be
much healthier as a society if we could convince each
person to strive toward a process of life long growth and
change.

Perhaps the most effective way to teach children to
risk, to grow, and to change would be to provide an
example for them. To teachers everywhere I would say,
"Grow, risk, stretch out, make mistakes, and fail from
time to time." When teachers demonstrate how we learn
from our shortcomings and mistakes, students will have
permission to do the same.

During my first term teaching at Western Michigan University in Kalamazoo, Michigan, I committed myself to a change. I would learn to swim.

All of my childhood years were spent in southern Minnesota, and access to swimming pools was limited. Once each week during the summer months, a group of young boys and girls gathered in front of our elementary school, we boarded a school bus, and were taken to the pool in a nearby community for swimming lessons. At eight-thirty in the morning the water in the pool was cold. I had been overly protected for years by a mother who imposed strong rules to insure her first child's safety. Each time I entered that cold water I gasped, inhaled cold water into my breathing mechanism, and choked. My mind filled with many of the thoughts I'd been taught, such as "—don't go near the water, you'll drown." My well developed fear of water turned junior and senior high school outings to camps or to the swimming holes into nightmares to be avoided at all costs. I did not conquer my fear of the water and I did not learn to swim.

When I chose to major in physical education as an undergraduate, I was aware that the program required me to take at least one swimming course. After much diligence and several frightening experiences, I learned these two things: 1) that I could put my face under water and survive, and 2) I could dog paddle long enough to maneuver my body to shallow water or the edge of the pool.

At age thirty five and living in Kalamazoo, Michigan, with my family including four children who were very comfortable in the water, I made a commitment to learn to swim. We joined the YMCA. I practiced in my bathtub and at the "Y" pool. I progressed rapidly and was ready to perform the final test, to go off the diving board, swim to the edge and live to tell the story. "This Sunday night, if there's no one else in the pool I'll make my dive," I promised my two older children.

The pool was empty save members of my family. I was nervous. Chris and Carrie were exhilarated. I walked cautiously to the end of the board, bounced ever so slightly and dived, head first, into the water. The force of my entry into the water pulled my swim trunks down about my ankles. Under the water I struggled with that wet suit, pulled it into place and managed to get to the edge safely. Oh, how we laughed.

To share a risk taking experience with members of my class at Western Michigan University seemed appropriate in hopes they would know the value of teaching by example. I chose to use the first few minutes of class time to tell my story. I will confess to some over-dramatization as I shared the details of my trial dive. Most members of the teacher education group were laughing and vicariously enjoying the tale of my experience. Two young ladies sitting in the front row, stood out by their non-response. I suspected they wanted to be noticed and so I teased them a bit and asked them if they had enjoyed the story.

They burst into laughter and almost simultaneously blurted out, "Oh, we enjoyed it very much as we watched from behind the glass at the "Y" last night.

Parents, teachers, and all people responsible for our children's development can use examples from their own lives to assist children to approach growth and change with confidence and self assurance. On the other hand, our example to children might produce behaviors which cause later discomfort or difficulty for the child. The example given some children and the subsequent learning might cause those around the child discomfort.

I had absolutely no question in my mind that I could change those seventh grade students assigned to my classes. I was considerably bigger than they were, spoke better than they did, and had power granted by the school board to grade every child who walked into my room. In my excellent teacher preparation program, I had heard about changing behavior. We were taught that one way to measure learning was to note changes in behavior and then infer that the child had learned.

For several years this theory seemed to work, then came Russell. Russell had triple B.O. He had body odor, he had breath odor, and he had barn odor. They were so neatly mixed together that people couldn't tell where one ended and another began. None of the other students would sit by Russell and when asked about their avoidance behavior several would complain, "He breathes on me!"

Based upon my learning I reasoned, "I'll change Russell this year as I'm so dynamic and so alive."

Many of you know that in our secondary schools, odor isn't in the English department—physical education teachers deal with odor; English teachers work with speech and writing. One of Russell's speech habits was particularly unacceptable and perplexing. Russell began every sentence with the word, "Goddammit!" The repeated use of this word was totally inappropriate and offensive to me so my change plan was put into place.

We were alone in the hallway as I spoke to him, "You won't be able to say that word in my room, Russell. I'm offended by the word and so are these other people in this room."

Russell's speech was appropriate for twenty minutes and he slipped back, so he was reminded of the admonition. A bit later when Russell slipped back he was threatened, "Russell, say it outdoors if you must, or say it in the restroom, but not in my room, you understand." The third violation occurred and Russell was told, "If you say that one more time, you'll stay after school and your parents will be called."

In the middle of the spelling test that afternoon, I pronounced the word "buffalo." Russell's voice was barely audible yet very clear saying, "Goddammit, I can't remember if there's one 'f' or two."

"That's it, Russell, you'll stay after school tomorrow night. Tell your parents to come in to get you."

Preparations were made in that room the next afternoon. I'd put air-wick on the desk. I'd opened the window and moved the chair over next to the window hoping Russell would sit there.

Immediately after last hour, he came into my room appearing much too happy for a child forced to remain after school. He grabbed the chair, pushed it close to me, pressed his knees into my thigh, and he breathed right on me. Do you know how long forty-five minutes is? "Is his mother never coming?"

A tall woman appeared in the doorway. Her hair was unkempt, her face plain and dirty, her work clothes showed the signs of the chores she'd done, and her shoes looked like she had just walked in out of the barn. I'm quite sure the words came out automatically, "You must be Russell's mother."

She looked at me with no smile or pleasantness in sight and firmly stated, "Goddammit, this had better be worthwhile."

The words slipped so easily out of my mouth, "This conference is over."

"The hell it is," she shouted. She jerked her son forward and demanded, "You tell this man your schedule."

Russell had obviously been coached. "I get up at five in the morning and go down to the barn to help my dad. If nothing goes wrong, we finish the chores at about seven-thirty. I don't bother to go back to the house," he continued. (I thought to myself, 'I wouldn't either if that woman lived there.') "I get on the bus and get to school at eight-thirty. At three-thirty we leave school and I'm back home at four-thirty. I stop to help Dad and if we don't have trouble we finish the chores at eight-thirty. I go into the house, get something to eat and I go straight to bed, 'cause goddammit, five o'clock comes awfully early in the morning."

I knew that I couldn't work a schedule like that

and that he probably had to do this every day of the week. He probably saw school as a resting place. I also know the source of his language specialty. At that point mother pointed her finger at me and scolded, "If Russell should do something in the future to displease you, you kick him, you hit him, you do what you have to to get him to do your thing, but goddammit, don't keep him after school."

It was no problem to promise her that I would never keep Russell after school as I didn't want her back in my office. I taught Russell how to live, how to learn and how to laugh.

Years later I returned to that area to teach a class in that school. I would now teach the teachers with whom I'd previously taught. I was early for my first class and as I approached the restaurant to get a bite to eat, I noticed an adolescent male standing on the street outside the cafe. I had no idea who this young man was, until he spoke, "Well, goddammit, Kern, I haven't seen you for a long time!"

When the boy moved in close I had no doubt about who he was, Russell had grown up. He's married now and farming quite a parcel of land including the farm of his parents and doing quite well. Russell and his new wife have three little boys. They smell just like Russell smelled; they talk just as Russell talked; and they all know the value of hard work.

To be a parent or teacher demands that we live as we would have our children live.

Another valuable insight into changing can be gained by considering the frustration, disappointment, and despair of many people who continue to believe that one person can change another. Many young people get married with the firm belief that they will be able to change their partners after marriage. At least two points need to be presented to these young people: 1) If your goal is to change a self destructive behavior, you will be accused at some point of being the cause of the behavior. Should you, then, accept any responsibility for this, you are probably just as much in need of help as your partner; and 2) If you are successful in bringing forth a change, you may find that you loved the person as he/she was more than the person you've helped create.

So let's review some of the things we've considered in this area. We can change ourselves, it's called growth. We very likely can not change others. Children need models to follow. If you've agreed with those things, here's an invitation to consider a change for your life — today.

Over the past few years largely as a result of this nation's emphasis on personal wellness, many suggestions have been advanced to increase both the quality and the length of one's life. Over and over five areas of growth are recommended. The invitation comes like this: " Would you like to add on average eleven years to your life?" If you answer YES, then you will need to find a way to incorporate these five things into your life.

When I first encountered these ideas for adding an extra eleven years to my life, I thought about how nice the time would be especially in light of my love for my children, but I reasoned, "I'm so busy now; I'll do these things when I have time." Have you ever reasoned this way? To take advantage of this offer for an extra eleven years, you'll have to 'pay now' to 'fly later.'

What are those five things we must incorporate into our behavior if we are to enjoy those additional eleven years? Let's look them over and as we do, what commitments could you make to yourself for making changes in your life?

1) If you want to add eleven years to your life, you will not smoke at all. The evidence continues to come forth that smoking is harmful not only to the smoker, but to all those around the smoker, especially little children. To respect the clean air requests of non-smokers, the smokers change their smoking habits, for example, they go outside or to specific areas, or postpone smoking until later. This change will help others to live longer; now, smokers, consider a more selfish concern. Dropping this habit requires tremendous effort, an effort which begins with a commitment to growth.

2) If you want to add eleven years to your life and you use alcohol, you must use it moderately or less. The misuse and abuse of this drug still ranks as number one amongst the harmful drugs. Also because alcohol is so easily accessible and socially acceptable, the dangers mount. Under the influence of alcohol people continue to function as if nothing has changed. In fact the potential hurt to many others has escalated considerably. As with smoking, a change here will appreciably improve the quality of life for those around the drinker. The next step again is to be selfish, curtail the misuse and abuse for your own health.

3) If you want to add eleven years to your life, you must diet religiously. I've asked audiences to think about dieting in light of these questions: 1) How many of you have learned that you can diet and gain weight? 2) How many of you believe that being thin doesn't need to be the only reason to diet? and 3) How many of you know someone who isn't particularly thin who seems to be a grand person? I am convinced we should begin teaching our children, through our words and our examples, that dieting means eating the right foods, in the right quantities, at the right times. This could very well reduce the pressure on very young people to begin severe diets.

4) If you want to add eleven years to your life, you must exercise four times a week. "Impossible," you say. "With my schedule, there's no time for exercise." Those who follow a regular exercise regimen of twenty to thirty minutes per day for four days per week report many benefits among them more energy, less stress, better sleep patterns, and improved eating habits. To walk briskly, swinging your arms vigorously, and carrying along weights when you're ready to advance in the program, will strengthen your heart as well as tone your muscles.

5) If you want to add eleven years to your life, you will always fasten your seat belts. We have in Texas a seat belt law requiring people to fasten their belts. I have never believed that a law would be necessary; instead I believed that common sense and a little love would motivate people to have that belt in place at all times when the vehicle is moving. The message which has compelled me to fasten my belt forever was the commercial with the child walking along a fence row, hitting the posts, and speaking directly into the camera. He hit that first post saying, "I wish everyone would wear their (sic) seat belts." He hit the second post without saying a word allowing the viewer to think about the message. As he hit the third he said, "I sure (sic) wish my parents would have fastened theirs." The fourth was hit as the second one, in silence, giving the viewer a chance to think through what had been said. Then he hit the last and spoke, "I'm living with my grandparents now." Then the child stopped and a voice over the picture said, "If you love your children, you'll fasten your seat belt."

Principle # 5

HOW WE FEEL IS AS IMPORTANT AS WHAT WE KNOW.

Can this be possible? Is he saying that how people feel is as important as what they know? Hasn't knowledge and its understanding brought us to this standard of living which we all enjoy? Yes, I believe that how a person feels influences directly the possibilities for using our knowledge. From some of my acquaintances, questions like this will surface, "Don't you want the pilot on your airplane to know a lot about flying the plane?" Of course, I do want anyone with control over my life and welfare to know a lot—and I want each one to feel really good about self and others.

No person needs to live the life of an educated fool. People who grow in wisdom realize the importance of what my father called 'common sense' and also the importance of compassion. My hope for all people would be that they grow toward the good life, acquiring as much information and knowledge as is possible and learning the importance of feeling good.

Throughout our lives, and especially in the early developmental years, negative feelings or trauma can effectively block the learning process. Conditions exist in the lives of some children which make the acquisition of information difficult if not impossible. Many youngsters experience elements of failure, embarrassment, hurt, rejection, neglect or abuse. Much of their energy must be spent in surviving, and therefore, they have little energy left for learning.

I further believe that many people in addition to parents, teachers, and school administrators and counselors influence how a child feels. Some of these people are labeled "non-professional", still they contribute much to the education of children if we truly believe that how a child feels is important. Janitors, bus drivers, food service people, secretaries, and instructional aides contribute so much to our children's learning and often receive little recognition. In industrial settings the support people serve to create a more pleasant work environment, and wise employers regularly recognize their contributions in a number of ways.

The caller to our home, a school superintendent, wants to arrange an inservice training session for a school staff and we ask that the classified personnel be included. Frequently we hear statements like these: 1) "We've never done that before," 2) "I've never even thought of that," 3) "They have meetings in their own departments," or 4) "We can't afford to have them there."

I dream of the day when these most important people are invited to and included in all training sessions for those who work with children. Many parents will testify to the importance of the support staff in recalling early school experiences. Do you remember your child's first trip to the school?

> When Chris came home after his first day in kindergarten, he marched into the house and announced, "Dad, from now on in our house, we'll walk up the stairs on the right hand side and down the stairs on the right hand side."
> "What in the world are you talking about?"
> "Well," he said, "Mrs. Foss told us, 'If the building catches on fire, we don't want any collisions on the stairway.'" I didn't have the heart to tell him that if the building were on fire, no one would be going up!
> Carrie ran home one year later, burst into the house, and exclaimed, "Dad, do you know what happened in our school?"
> "No, what happened?"
> "We had a fire drill," she said. "Do you know what that is, Dad? A buzzer rings and everybody runs outside. Dad, the building wasn't burning, it was just pretend. But the kindergartners were so-o lucky—before the buzzer rang, God came on to tell us where to go." (The principal had announced the drill over the intercom to these youngest of our students.)

Picture another five year old practicing going to school for the very first time. He gathers his things and practices going to school for several days in advance. When the big day arrives, this excited young boy will kiss Mom, run to the curb, and wait for the arrival of the school bus. Mom is watching from the window thinking, "Oh dear, he'll be dirty even before the bus comes."

The appearance of the bus fills the child with new fears: it's so big—the action of the doors is totally unfamiliar—it's nearly full of unfamiliar people. The child will stand in awe and wonder in front of that open door and will hear a male voice saying, "Get in! Sit down! and Shut up!"

The boy will get in, he will sit down, and he'll not make a sound; but this experience will live with the child throughout this day. What will he learn in school today? Who is taking him home tonight? When he's safely back home he'll cling to his mother and share, "Mom, I don't think I want to go back to school tomorrow."

Mom will picture in her mind an awful teacher. In this case it's not the teacher at all; it's the first person from the school to touch our kids in the morning and the last to touch our kids at night. This is a person we often label "non-professional" and exclude from our training meetings. Do any of you agree that our bus drivers may possibly have the toughest job in America? How many of us could handle the responsibility of fifty to sixty kids, ranging in age from five to eighteen, sitting down, with our backs to them, and something in our hands which means life or death to them all?

With over one thousand high school kids in the auditorium, I'll ask, "How many of you believe that the school cook influences how you feel?"

The response can be quite loud and animated so I continue, "—and, how many of you believe that you might influence how the cook feels?" Hopefully, some become aware of the important contribution these people make.

The school cook works hard in the school to help meet the needs of children, one of the most basic needs, the need for food. For many youngsters, the meal they receive in the school lunch program may be the only nourishing meal eaten in a day. Still, the cook often receives more than his/her share of negative feedback. Through it all the cooks create as much joy and laughter in many schools as all other groups combined.

A woman dressed in white greeted me inside the door of a small elementary school in the northeast. I assumed I knew what her role was, so after a greeting I asked, "Why do you cook for this school?"

Her answer surprised me and took me aback. Her tone was unusually loud and her tone was harsh, "Because my husband died!" Since her answer didn't seem appropriate to my question, I thought to myself that this woman could not hear.

"Your husband died?"

"Yes, when he died, I needed a job. I knew how to cook, and I knew how to clean, and I didn't want to clean." I was nervous in her presence. I excused myself and went to the teacher's lounge.

During that morning as I worked with a variety of people, students, parents, and teachers, I remember many people saying that the cook was "—very good with kids," and that I must "—watch her give the food to them at lunch. It's a miracle," they repeated over and over again.

Even though I was still nervous, I stood right beside her during that lunch period to watch the miracle I'd been promised. She knew the name of every child and she called each in turn by name: "Hello, Billy, how are you? - David, you missed a week. Are you better now, dear? - Mark, how's your new dog?"

Then came Sally, with no front teeth, holding her plate high. The cook spoke loudly and clearly, "How many peas do you want, Sally?"

"One," the child replied.

I watched the cook take that large spoon, reach deeply into the kettle just as she had done for all the other youngsters, and when she raised that spoon, there was one pea rolling back and forth in the bottom. She placed it on the child's plate saying, "Be sure you eat it all!"

Sally walked off with a big smile and the cook winked at me.

Sally will very likely eat the pea, and if she should increase the number in her request, she may learn to like peas. In our homes we often place food on the children's plates and then admonish them to "—sit right here until it's all gone!"

How many of you parents remember a time when
you hid food you didn't like? How many have sneaked
the food off the table into the mouth of a pet? How
many remember your mother saying, "—think of all the
poor starving people —?"

Finally, think about those people who spend day
after day cleaning our work areas so that tomorrow's
environment is inviting. The results of a job well done
effects all of us, yet we often forget to recognize their
worth and the value of their contribution.

I left the room with the energetic and unpredict-
able second graders to observe them and their supervisor during recess. Their energy and their total lack of
inhibition were both fascinating and amusing.

The custodian of the school walked across the play
area. One confident little fellow shouted loudly to the
large man, "Hey, Mister, my desk squeaks!" The older
man glanced over at the child and at the teacher and
went about his business.

Shortly after we had returned to the room, the
same custodian knocked and entered the room with a
large oil can in one hand, a twinkle in his eyes, and his
loud bass voice filling the air, "Where's that boy with
the squeaky desk?" The child, not nearly so confident
now, raised his hand. The custodian walked quickly
toward the child and asked him to stand out of the
way. He squirted oil on the desk. As I watched, I
thought to myself that the oil had been placed in a non-
moving place, it will do no good. "Sit down," the older
man commanded. The desk squeaked loudly and the
boy moved out of the way again. More oil, more
squeaks, more oil, more squeaks and finally the
squeaky joint received the necessary lubrication. The
children breathed easier as the desk remained silent.

"Let's show this man that we're happy he came to
our room," the teacher encouraged, and everyone
applauded. He left and the young teacher continued,
"He's made our room more pleasant, hasn't he?" A
chorus of "Yes!" filled the air. "What could we do to
make his work more pleasant?"

The second graders began slowly, but as soon as

they made the connec-
tion between this man
and a clean school, they
needed to be heard.
Each response was
printed on the chalk-
board.

We could:
—pick up the paper on
the floor.
—clean off the board.
—keep our gum off. (sic)
—put up the chairs.
—turn off the lights.

One little girl
suggested, "We could
write him a love note on
the board so he could
read it when he comes
in to work." The teacher seemed especially excited at
this suggestion. A schedule was prepared which provided each child a time in which his or her note would
be printed on the board by the teacher.

Several weeks later this little note appeared in my
mail box:

Dear Jim Kern,

We've been writing our 'love notes' on the board at
the end of every day. My room is cleaner every morning
than it's ever been before. I haven't heard any com-
plaints about our duck-chick hatching area and just
lately we come into our room in the morning to read a
return note from our new friend—the janitor.

Love,
The Second Graders

Part II

Basic Needs
of People

BUILD THE FORT...TODAY!

What do we need to stay alive and well? Answers provided for this question give insight into the vocation or maybe the value system of the responding person. The teacher, having heard many voices demanding that education must get back to basics, will suggest that the "Three R's", reading, 'riting, and 'rithmetic are necessary. Others, the politicians, the economists, the farmers, or the businessmen, may provide a slightly different list of basic needs. Each of us in our own way suggests needs which must be met before people can be expected to grow, to reach beyond their places, to accomplish, to know, or to be fulfilled.

Having been a teacher for most of my life, I would address those needs educators have considered basic to our children and the challenge today's teacher faces from an ever demanding public. I believe that we have never left the teaching of "the basics" in education. We have explored new ways to teach these basic skills, and some have proved more effective than others. I believe that having these skills is essential for continuing growth in our high tech world. Illiterate people certainly work at a tremendous disadvantage. Those who do not understand even the most fundamental mathematics principles will be handicapped in today's world. And while many people write nothing after their formal educational experience, a case could easily be made for the importance of writing.

Having said that, let me suggest an informal title for this section of my work and at the same time share what I believe to be "More Basic Than the Basics." People will survive if they are unable to read, write, and do arithmetic. The absence of these skills will not threaten our existence. On many occasions I've used a bit of deception to reinforce a point from my beliefs presentation. "How many of you know at least one human being who doesn't read, write, or do arithmetic, but who seems to be doing quite well?"

A few raise their hands immediately and after very serious thought other hands appear. "For those of you who didn't raise your hand, think of a human being who is less than two years old." Most very young children have none of these skills, yet they're doing very well and learning very much and very fast.

So, what are the needs of all human beings which are so basic that without them we will not survive? What are those needs which we might call "More Basic Than All the Basics"? What are the essential elements which will need to be in place before a person can give any attention to reading, writing, or arithmetic? I'll be using information from my own life as well as from the writings of several people to identify four needs which I believe are the most essential. As in the case of my beliefs in the previous section, I've not placed these needs in order of their importance. All of us needs each of these, or each of us needs all of these, whichever you prefer.

Need #1

AFFECTION

Without love and affection in their lives people will shrivel up and die. Consider how universal this is as I look at different age groups of people in our world.

Infants die without love. On many occasions when I've spoken these words a young mother's eyes will be cast downward. She'll often cover her mouth with her hand, and the tears may flow. After the meeting she might share that she lost her child to sudden infant death syndrome. She heard me say that babies die without love, her baby died, and for a moment her guilt overwhelms her. Much evidence can be accumulated now to correct her mistaken belief. SIDS babies do not die from a lack of affection.

Adolescents die without affection. To stimulate thinking with a smile I've frequently raised three questions to people who experience adolescents. 1) "How many of you believe that adolescents need love?" Many hands go up here. 2) "How many of you know that they can sometimes be hard to love?" Hands fly up high as people laugh with insights and enthusiasm. 3) "And how many of you know that this is normal?" Most settle back at this point and nod, realizing that one of the developmental tasks of adolescence is to pull away, to establish themselves as independent beings. During this period, these kids are experiencing many other changes as well as declaring their independence, and they can become very difficult to love. Many times they can't even find much in themselves to love.

Older people die without love and affection. I'm often hurt, angry, and embarrassed when I see how some of our seniors are treated in this society. Too often these folks are put away in a place where we visit them only at our convenience, and in increasing numbers of instances, they are bilked, cheated, and hurt by younger people. For most of my life, my grandmother and grandfather served as my examples for how older people live.

He always called her Momma and his love for her was obvious. Grandma and Grandpa Kern were married and they lived together for fifty six years and two months. All of the relatives knew that he would do anything for her and that her life was dedicated to working with him to create a happy, successful and fun-loving family.

Toward the end of her life she had to take a special "medicine" for her heart. She didn't like it at all so she called it medicine. My grandfather liked it so he called it what it was—Whiskey. Out of respect for her, however, he always called it medicine when he spoke to her saying, "Momma. I'll get your medicine." He would go to the kitchen alone and would be gone for a long time.

She quizzed me several times asking, "Jim, I take only one teaspoon of that medicine in the morning and one tablespoon in the evening. That fifth is gone in three days; do you think it evaporates?" Her eyes betrayed the mischief in her question.

Late summer provided my grandparents an opportunity to sit on the western exposure porch watching all neighborhood activity and commenting on all of the passers by. I would guess that he told Momma that he'd get her medicine and that he left the porch for a long time. Upon returning he very likely believed that she had dozed off for a bit. He spoke to her. No answer. He spoke again.

He realized after touching her that she wasn't living in there any more. He didn't know how to use modern conveniences, but he was able to get help from his children nearby. An ambulance was called and her body was taken away. Her funeral was one of the saddest I've ever attended.

The next few months were extremely hard for him.

I visited often and received some special remembrance of Momma each time. Her cake pans, a special spatula, her bread pans and special dishes were presented always with much sorrow and a story about her and how much he missed her. The autumn holidays were very difficult. Hardest of them all was Christmas, which found him missing her even more when gifts were opened and each one contained a special reminder of her.

In a very short time, he could tolerate the loneliness no longer, and he went to the hospital. He made his wishes known to anyone who would listen. He didn't want to be here, he just wanted to be with Momma. Grandpa left this earth on Grandma's birthday, January 20, 1962, exactly seventy-five years after her birth.

Affection, so necessary to life, can be hard to acquire. If I needed money, I would seek a loan, I would ask for it and would usually get it. On one occasion I was working with senior high school student council members in Iowa. I asked a young woman if she would loan me ten dollars if I were in a pinch. She said that she would and later, she came quietly to me with a ten dollar bill tucked into her palm asking if I really needed money. If we needed food, we would ask and we would receive it. But, how does someone ask for affection? Children of all ages have used these and other techniques through the years to get affection: attention getting devices, power trips, mischief or vandalism, disobedience, acting out, and even a variety of self-destructive behaviors. These negative behaviors often prove to be self-defeating, empty, and hurtful, still the negative response they will certainly elicit is frequently interpreted as better than no response or attention at all.

To simply ask for affection remains a very difficult assignment. I spend much of my life now in airports around the world. Many times the love my wife and family have for me seems far away. As I walk down the concourse, I notice a very pleasant woman. What do you imagine might happen if I were to approach her and say, "I really need affection?"

Asking for love or affection can be further complicated as we remember one of the lessons learned in childhood. I was taught as a youngster that good boys don't ask for the things they need or want.

> "Good boys don't ask for what they want." The lesson was repeated many times during my childhood. We were to sit quietly and politely"—to be seen not heard," we were told. The message still lives with me and occasionally operates outside my consciousness.
>
> Mother would turn to her children in the back seat of our car on the way to grandparents' homes for holidays and she would admonish us with these words: "Now don't you ask Grandma for food!" or "Don't you ask Grandpa to get those toys out!" The message was very clear: DON'T ASK FOR WHAT YOU WANT!!

Apparently we were to wait until someone guessed
what it was we wanted. Secretly, we knew Grandma
would get us some of our favorite foods, Grandpa
wasn't so reliable with those special toys.

Sometimes as an adult I wait for people to guess
what I want and later blame them if my needs are not
appropriately met.

So how do we meet this important need if we can't
ask? Over and over again in my lifetime one lesson has
been repeated. I may finally be learning the importance
of the lesson now that I'm past fifty years old. I frequently sat with my parents in the pew at church.

When my large strong father announced that we
would be going to church, his children had no choice. I
clearly remember my aversion to going "—be quiet, —
sit still, —be polite." The sessions seemed awfully long
to a child and the sermon seemed to be the worst part
of the service. So often the message wasn't relevant to
anything in my experience and no one else partici-
pated, and no one laughed.

From the pulpits I heard our pastors saying, "It's
more blessed to give than to receive." The theme found
its way into nearly every stewardship service, but as a
youngster I just listened to the words and internalized
them at face value. This created a big conflict inside
me. Giving, I reasoned, must become a part of my life.
This would make me a blessed person. I would be
rewarded for sharing even though much in my experience screamed against giving. Receiving, I thought,
must be avoided at all costs. By receiving graciously I
would be less blessed, less "good"; however, in my mind
I knew how happy I became when I received something
I desired.

Today the simplistic reasoning of the child surfaces
along with the conflict. To a compliment, I might
respond with embarrassment and an explanation. On
receiving a gift, I often hear myself saying, "Oh, you
shouldn't have done this!"

I'm past fifty years now and the mystery of that
early lesson seems more clear. Giving and receiving are
the same thing—they are synonymous. We give and are

filled with immeasurable joy. Recapture the joy and satisfaction you felt as you watched a little child open a gift you've presented—in giving you have received. As you receive the gift of another graciously and enthusiastically, you allow each one to know those same feelings.

Giving is receiving and receiving is giving.

Each of us needs to receive affection. Is it possible that we can take the responsibility for meeting our own need by applying the lesson? Could we actually fulfill our own needs for affection by giving it to others? I believe that each of us can learn to fill our own cups with affection. We need to experience giving without expectation of getting something back in return to know that we can meet our own need for affection.

Here are three relatively easy ways to give affection to others. Each of us can give these gifts often without additional cost of either money or excessive time.

1) WE GIVE AFFECTION TO OTHERS BY PAYING ATTENTION TO THEM.

Most of us enjoy being noticed. Perhaps the shy person in his or her own way seeks attention by acting shy. (I think 'shy' is something we **do** rather than something we **are**.) To notice something about another and bring it to his/her attention communicates caring in a most sincere way. When a woman changes her hair style, she would probably rather have a special someone notice and not like it than to not notice it at all. (Many women would like to have a third option.) Men want very much for significant others to notice even the slightest improvement on projects around the house. (I remember calling Denise and Carrie into the garage to notice one two by four I had postitioned on the floor as a part of my home improvement project.)

Young parents know that infants request attention. Ignoring those requests will create an even greater void in the child, and the child moves from request to demand. The demands can quickly become inappropriate and unacceptable. Parents become irritated and exhausted and the foundation for trouble exists. By anticipating the child's needs and noticing your baby even for a short time, you will often satisfy the child. The child having received this simple expression of affection will learn to be secure and content in the knowledge, "I am loved!" The parents will also have helped themselves through the giving of attention to the child.

Seventh graders vary tremendously in their behaviors designed to get attention. Teachers of this age group learn very quickly that many of their students have received very little attention and have monumental needs for affection. Other students in the same classes have received more and are reasonably secure. Nearly all kids in this age group, however, will radiate happiness when we notice something unique and positive about them. They may choose to alter their behaviors even to a point of danger when ignored.

Because she would join her family for a portrait to be used in the church directory at two-thirty, she wore her nicest dress to school. Throughout this January day she received understandable feedback on her lovely dress. I complimented her as I passed the six junior high school girls on my way to lunch. She was most gracious in her thank you and acceptance of the kind words she continued to receive.

Later in parent/teacher conferences, five mothers reported how their daughters had come home from school and related the incidents surrounding the compliments. Their daughters insisted that on the very next day, each of them would wear her very nicest dress. Mothers told of the preparations: the washing, the starching, the ironing, and the late hours this work required. Having observed the attention given their friend, these girls would now be positioned to receive the same kind words, the same looks.

The next morning the temperature fell to seventeen degrees below zero, and the wind blew in gusts up to twenty miles per hour. Wise mothers took daughters aside to explain the danger posed by this weather on exposed skin. Perhaps mothers used some version of this statement: "Just put some jeans on under your skirt. When you get into the school building, go imme-diately to the women's bathroom, slip your jeans off, and put them into your locker." Can't you just hear the fuss created by these young women?

Three of these young people, those who lived closest to the school, arrived at our school door that day with the beginnings of frostbite on the front of the exposed legs.

Whenever the opportunity arises for me to work with married couples, I suggest that husbands and wives use one another's names—especially in times without obvious upset or anger present. Using your spouse's name might arouse suspicions, but might also result in a deeper and more meaningful relationship.

Husbands and wives can demonstrate affection to one another in the simple act of using one another's names in conversation. All too often "Honey" marries "Sweetheart." Children appear and the names change to "Mommy" and "Daddy" to be followed much too quickly by "Grandma" and "Grandpa." People go to their graves never again hearing someone say, "Good night, Harold" or "Good night, Margaret."

Try it now. Call your spouse by his or her name and in this simple act tell him or her that you really care. (I have reminded people to get the right name, for goodness sakes.)

Denise and I were in bed and very angry with one another. Neither of us could go to sleep as we'd been taught, "Don't go to sleep angry." I'm lying on my side of the bed facing the wall with my back to her. She's on her side, back to me, facing opposite. "She's so stubborn!" I thought.

Between two and three in the morning, I'd pretty well forgotten the cause of the dispute. To bring peace to this relationship I called on the child part of me to reach across the space between us and sign off so we could each sleep. Do you remember how those two popular newscasters ended their news report? It's worth a try I thought, and in my best David Brinkley imitation I said, "Good night, Chet."

She turned toward me and giggled, "Good night, David." I've called her Chet ever since.

Using the acceptable name of another could also improve our relationships with business associates, supervisors, and with clients and customers. This man's art helped him and gave me a good laugh.

He owned and operated a service station in the suburbs and people liked to patronize his place partly because he would remember and use their names as he talked with his customers. He never forgot a name and he could call your name on your second visit. Even in casual conversation away from the station people marveled at his gift.

Dick had heard me tell of this man and when he moved to the suburb, he decided he'd test the man's ability. He drove into the station, ordered a full tank of gasoline, and handed the owner his credit card. The transaction was completed and Dick drove away formulating his plan. He would return ten days later to see if this rumor was true.

When that time came for the ultimate test, Dick drove his car into the station and was secretly pleased as he noticed the same man approach the car. The hose was taken from the pump, it was placed into the tank, and the gas flowed. The attendant walked by the car window and spoke, "Hello, Dick. How are you today?"

Dick was astounded. How does he remember my name? He had to ask. The attendant revealed one of his many secrets. "Remember when you gave me your credit card? I wrote your name on a small piece of masking tape and stuck it inside the gas cap."

And sometimes when we work so hard to get the name of a person right the result can be confusing as well as a bit funny.

The reading teachers who gathered together in the otherwise empty school house in northern Michigan on this Saturday morning were ready to work toward the development of new strategies for effectively teaching youngsters to read. I wanted to involve them in meaningful conversations rather than lecture at them for the six hour period we had scheduled. Quite early in the day, I directed my attention to a sixty-plus year old woman near the front of the room. I asked this hypothetical question: "Suppose you had in your class a child who gazed about the room, was obviously distracted, and spent time daydreaming. How would you reach this child?"

After waiting a reasonable time for a response, I wondered whether or not she had heard me. I moved closer to her and asked a second question, "What is your name?"

I was unaware that when she spoke to me, she was answering my first question. "Read a story," she said apprehensively.

Several times during the day I turned to her to ask such things as "—what do you think, Rita?" Each time she would turn and search behind her for someone named Rita.

On the way back to my home I learned that her name was not Rita Storie at all.

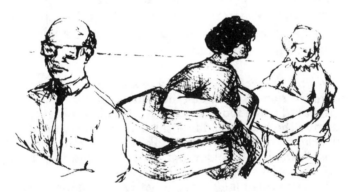

2) WE GIVE AFFECTION TO OTHERS BY TOUCHING THEM.

So much has been written and said about the power of touching. Children warm to touches from others. Patients feel the healing power of a touch and many of us enjoy a proper and affectionate touch. Early in my work as a speaker, I recommended that helpers become comfortable with touching and that they use the power of touch often, but carefully. More recently I've tempered my remarks in the face of increasing misunderstanding and the threats and realities of lawsuits if intentions are mis-read. Today I believe it behooves us all to be extremely cautious while using this powerful tool.

Many ways exist for me to touch another without making physical contact at all. In the next few paragraphs I'll present some ways each of us can touch others, and in touching, express our affection toward them.

More and more I'm aware of touching others with my words. Words have tremendous power to communicate caring as well as hurt and anger. Many children can vouch for the truth of the statement that words sometimes hurt more than a fist. We can put words in combinations which will bring tears to our eyes or laughter from our hearts. At no time in my life have I been more aware of the power of words than the night I spoke near Harrisburg, Pennsylvania.

We had expected about fifty to sixty people to attend the home-school meeting and were totally unprepared when four hundred ten people appeared. (Imagine the task of dividing the sixty cookies provided by the advisory council) As I walked to the front and looked to my left, an older man smiled. I knew that I should have been able to call him by name, but my mind was totally blank. I could not have said his name under threats of death.

Through the early part of my presentation, I relaxed behind the words to see if his name would come to me. One hour ten minutes into my talk I remembered him. He had been the placement director at Winona State University for many years. I had written to him in the late 1960's explaining that I would be leaving southern Minnesota to pursue a doctor's degree at the University of Wyoming. My final sentence was this request, "Would you help me find a teaching job within forty miles of Laramie, Wyoming?"

His answer came back reporting, "There's nothing but sagebrush within forty miles of Laramie, Wyoming."

My full attention was turned now to him and I asked, "Could you be Dr. Glen Fishbaugher?"

He stood ever so slowly—he was past eighty now—and spoke with no microphone, "I am. And I want you all to know that he's a hell of a lot better now than he was twenty years ago." Oh, how the audience laughed. He looked at me and asked, "Could I tell a story, too?"

I know I must always say "No" to old men and children, but I said "Yes." He began slowly:

A child came home from school and his mother asked him, "What did you learn in school?"

The child answered, "Nothing!"

Mother pressed on, "Didn't anything happen?"

"Well, there was a mouse in our room. He ran right up the teacher's leg. She grabbed him right about there. (He clutched his knee) And you should have seen all the water she squeezed out of that little mouse."

The people howled with laughter as he sat down. He had certainly touched my audience.

I've been there since and am thoroughly convinced that people come to the meetings hoping he'll share other stories to touch them again.

Touching other people with our eyes tells them we care. If you'll look into the eyes of a child, any aged child, you'll find the truth as children don't lie with their eyes. Skilled sales people learn to use their eyes effectively. Messages between lovers are transmitted through their eyes, and speakers know the importance of eye contact in reaching out to the members of the audience. I'm often aware of the perceived length of someone's presentation if the speaker chooses to read from a prepared text and refuses to touch the audience with his/her eyes.

We also touch people across time and miles with our thoughts. Throughout much of my lifetime people would offer these words as we parted company, "We'll keep you in our prayers." This way of touching someone remains as powerful today even if stated this way, "I'll be thinking of you."

My father played an important role in my development and I had become quite aware of the difficulty he had in expressing his feelings of affection and love for his male children especially. On the advice of people from my professional life, I found a unique way to touch my father before he died.

My father, a brick mason, loved his work and his family. Sunday afternoons found the family in the car touring places where he had built a step, a fireplace, a shopping center, or a hospital. We knew his stories by heart and as children would sit in the back seat and mimic him as he told his all too familiar stories. We all knew that he loved us, but that love wasn't easily and openly demonstrated. As children we learned to search through the laughter, through the sparkling eyes, through the teasing to find the love which nourishes. Talk about loving things, open expressions of love, touching and hugging seldom, if ever, entered into our relationships.

The advice came from good friends: you can touch your father before he dies. I heard several suggestions and chose to follow this one.

During Christmas time my family would spend Christmas day in my boyhood home. As we walked through that kitchen door on Christmas morning, my father would be somewhere else in the house—in the basement finishing a gift, in the bathroom, in front of the television set watching a sports event. I removed my outer wraps, walked into the living room, sat at the piano and began to play what I knew would be one of his favorite songs, "Mockingbird Hill". The smell of pipe tobacco announced his presence in the room; he placed his hand on my shoulder; he sang along and at the conclusion he said, "I like that. Could you play 'How Great Thou Art'?"

The notes came easily and he moved to the chair at my left. He's one of those remarkable people who could fall asleep in a few seconds. He was awake at the end saying, "How about 'What a Friend We Have in Jesus'." I kept playing and he continued his requests for about twenty five minutes until we were called to dinner. I

had touched my father.

He died very quickly a short time after that holiday and for quite a time, family members were painfully aware of his absence.

Years later when we returned to that home in southern Minnesota for Christmas, my dad wouldn't be there as we entered the house, but after all that had been the pattern. We entered the house, I removed my wraps, and once again went to the piano. When I began to play "Mockingbird Hill", I was sure I smelled the pipe tobacco; I could still feel that hand on my shoulder. In my mind he was right back there in that easy chair as I played "How Great Thou Art."

When we touch someone, really touch someone, the shared love lasts forever. It never ends.

By touching another in all of those ways each one of us can help others and improve ourselves at the same time. The relationships we create in which affection plays a central role will move us all toward a better world.

I've tried over the years to reach out to kids facing the loss of loved ones. When his grandmother became very ill, he stayed home to be with his family and therefore was absent from his ninth grade classes. I left my car engine idling in the street, I ran up to the door and rang the door bell. He came to the door with his mother so I had a chance to ask of his grandmother's progress and to offer any help the family might request. He especially wanted to introduce me to grandmother so I walked into the makeshift bedroom and spoke briefly to her. I received very little response from this very sick woman.

Her death and her funeral brought an end to a difficult time for the family and before long things returned pretty much to normal.

Several years later, I accepted an invitation to speak at a father and son banquet in southern Minnesota. I arrived early at the church and walked into the relatively dark and empty church basement. My mind was making cursory assessments about the location of speakers, location of posts which might obstruct someone's line of sight, position of head table and the order of business.

He stood in a dark corner somewhat hidden by a large post with his hand in the hand of his little boy. He seemed so proud of his son and so happy to have a chance for me to meet his boy. After the introductions he paused, thought a bit, and then spoke of times past. He did not mention his role in helping the school football team toward

the winning of a conference championship. He did not mention his important role in our student government. He did not say, "Remember all the fun we had with prepositions in English class?" He spoke clearly and with a touch of melancholy, "Do you remember the day you stopped at my house when my grandmother was sick?"

3) WE GIVE AFFECTION TO OTHERS WHEN WE LISTEN TO THEM.

Have you noticed that there are always more people who want to tell, to share, than there are people to listen? By listening to another we communicate affection, we assign importance to the message as well as to the person, and we create a relationship which can last indefinitely.

To listen with our ears brings us approximately ten percent of the message. To listen with our eyes and with our hearts allows us to hear more completely the true message of the sender. Listening skills can be learned and then practiced frequently in our lives.

What better way could there be to tell your children you love them than to listen to them? Children ask for a very small portion of our undivided attention and providing the time to listen when they ask will help the child in many ways. So often we get busy doing our own things and miss opportunities to grow closer to our kids through mutual sharing.

On January second in the Fiesta Bowl, two outstanding football teams would meet for the mythical national title. I watched intently as the Heisman Trophy winner displayed his talents leading his team against the old master coach and his well prepared athletes. I wasn't going to miss even one small part of the action on this day.

Three year old Katie came up beside me and said, "Daddy."

"Yes, Katie, what do you want?" I hadn't even

taken my eyes from the screen.

She climbed up onto the couch beside me and spoke quite urgently, "Daddy!"

"Tell me, Katie, I'm listening." The score was 14-13 with time running out. What a game!!

I felt her little hands on my cheeks. She pulled my face around toward her and she scolded, "Listen me with your eyes, Daddy."

How lucky we are that we can learn from the children in our lives. Having worked with pre-service education for teachers, in-service education and counselor education programs, and having taught listening skills in each of these settings, I believed that I understood the skill and that I did practice what I taught. A little child came into my life in a special way and taught me much more about love and listening.

I don't work very often any more with little children, so when I get the chance I literally jump at it. At an elementary school in the northern part of the United States on a cold January morning, I would have the opportunity to address every child in the kindergarten through eighth grade. In preparation for the first assembly the room was filled with sixth, seventh, and eighth graders. Several of the teachers and guests of the school had speculated over coffee about what behaviors we might expect. We were all pleasantly surprised when the student behaviors were most appropriate. They listened, they responded, and they asked questions.

The second assembly was comprised of grades three, four and five. They, too, were very polite,"— well behaved—" their teachers would report.

The kindergarten, first and second grade children came to the media center for the last assembly and all of us wondered if we would get that same exemplary behavior from this age group.

They sat on the floor, smushed together, surrounded by a forest of their teachers, and as I walked before them they had to believe I was enormous. I began with these words, "I've come today to make you happy." Every head went up just a bit; they began to talk to one another and the teachers in unison said, "Sh-h-h-h-h." This pattern was repeated again and again for thirty minutes.

The kids demonstrated that they could listen appropriately to a speech, that they could sit for thirty minutes, and that they could easily recognize the different feelings in adults even before the adults spoke to them. I finished this third presentation with words which seemed so appropriate, "Now, go from this room, find someone you love and say 'I love you.'"

Instantly I became aware that one must never say those words to little children. They came forward like an army of ants each one wanting to touch me and wanting at the same time to be touched; each one wanting that moment of attention—that touch which says, "I care!"; each one needing that moment when an adult listens to a child and in listening says, "I love you."

I was on my knees, fighting to keep my balance in the middle of the crowd when I noticed her. She was so little—about twenty-nine inches tall; she wore thick glasses; and she stood back a bit from the group almost as if she knew that she didn't fit into this class. I moved toward her. She placed her little arms about my neck, she squeezed me hard, and in a soft sweet gentle

voice whispered into my ear, "Jim, I'm Tina, and I
really love you." She went on to talk about herself. The
sharing and the listening created a special relationship
in a very short time. She then said the words to
which I could not respond, "Jim,
I'm going to die in May."

I held her briefly in my arms.
How hard it was to know what to
say! How impossible it was to
keep my self separate from her
pain! I recalled several other
times in my life when I was
privileged to be near someone at
the moment of intense hurt and
pain.

I did not see her again even
though she's often in my mind.
Her memory, the love she
shared in just a moment, and the
affirmation of loving through listening go
with me now everywhere I travel. Sometimes
when I'm alone and lonely, her spirit reap-
pears and I'm reminded of the important
lesson she taught me—that when we spend
time to listen to one another—really listen to
one another with our ears, with our eyes,
and with our hearts—we are each one filled
with affection.

Need # 2

FOOD

Food is only one of the physiological needs requiring satisfaction in order that we might survive. Along with such things as rest, protection from the elements, and sexual gratification, we need to be able to acquire food and consume it to stay alive and well. Used properly, food serves as a fuel to keep us going.

People have learned to abuse food in a variety of ways. Food is primarily a source of nourishment, and affection also provides us a type of nourishment. How many of you have been 'hungry' for affection and consumed food as a substitute? Just as we have learned to abuse alcohol and work as substitutes for other needs, we can abuse food.

High school students will admit to eating when they're bored, eating when they're lonely, and eating when they're watching televisions. Then when they date, food plays a central part in many of their activities. Food also plays a large role in the social lives of people well beyond the dating of adolescence. Think of the number of times we are invited to have a cup of coffee with someone only to discover that the coffee comes with high calorie and unnecessary food. It's entirely possible that you're eating something you just don't need at all as you're reading these words at this moment.

When and where did we learn to use food as a substitute for love and affection? I believe that for many of us these lessons were placed long before we were aware of having choices.

She was only three days old and she was busy waving her arms, kicking her legs and squawking loudly. A first time mother wanted her baby to be comfortable. She interpreted the crying as a call for help, not aware that the child may be exercising and communicating. She checked the tiny diaper. It was clean and dry. The child must be hungry, mother reasoned. She brought to her daughter a breast or a bottle providing comfort through food. For the baby, the basis of the lesson may now have taken root, "—when I have food in my tummy, my upsets leave, and I am loved."

She was three years old and playing in her own front yard with her own toys when the neighbor children snatched her toys away. She burst into tears, ran into the house and sobbed, "Mommy, I'm hungry." Mother, once again wanting to comfort her child, brought her little girl into the house and fed her. The earlier lesson is now reinforced, "—food removes my upsets." Mother might better have asked, "Hungry for a hug or a cookie?"

She was six years old and making her first trip to first grade in a new school. When she arrived at the front door of her room she became painfully aware of her ninety six pounds and of how much larger she was. She lacked the energy and the agility to participate in the typical activities of her classmates. They called her names, the names hurt, and she found comfort in food once more.

She was sixteen years old when she came to my office to inquire about dating problems. I knew her as a very bright, very pleasant, and physically very large young woman. An adult recognizes the beauty in this large girl, but the standards for date selection among sixteen year old boys can be excruciatingly exacting. I suspected she would not be chosen. My suspicions were

confirmed when I learned that she had not even been included in the parties which were very popular during the middle years. She casually described her "snacking" habits and I learned that her mother fed her family a diet of high calorie food and encouraged the children to eat heartily and not waste.

I called her family's doctor to arrange for a physical examination and I secretly hoped we'd get a reasonable diet for her. We met him together and he spoke forthrightly, "You know what your problem is—you're too fat."

When I registered shock at his direct statement, he told me that at times he found it easier "—to work with forty year old women filled up with cancer than sixteen year old girls who overeat." He clarified this by telling us that people with cancer will do whatever they're told to do. However, the sixteen year old who's upset or hurt will almost always sneak away to eat food. His eyes twinkled with mischief when he added, "—and they seldom sneak away with lettuce." (Be aware of the enjoyment you received the last time you sneaked off with a head of lettuce.)

This appetite mix-up occurs to many of us in subtle ways. Have you ever opened your refrigerator door, looked inside, and discovered that nothing looked good? Maybe you're not hungry for food at all. Perhaps another appetite needs satisfaction.

Food may be misused, substituted for affection, during those times in our lives when some expression of love from friends would be appreciated.

Many tragedies in our lives create in us a hunger which is satisfied best with expressions of love and affection, still many people choose to handle their own discomfort by substituting food.

My mother died when I was 14 years old. She had left our home to buy groceries for the weekend when a coronary thrombosis and cerebral hemorrhage took her away very quickly. We lived in a small village, everyone knew everyone else and many people wanted to express their feelings to a bereaved family, but instead of coming by to be with us, they brought food. Every

level surface in our kitchen was covered with food.
Many notes were lying near the baked goods, casse-
roles, and other foodstuffs. As I look back now I realize
I wasn't hungry
for food. I would
have preferred
that someone
hug me tightly
and let me cry.
The food would
not satisfy the
hunger I felt, and
since we had no way to store the food, much of it was
wasted.

In 1978 our house burned to the ground. We had
lost so much, and a nearby motel became our tempo-
rary home in the dark, cold morning. Early the next
day, a young couple came to our motel room to bring a
lovely dish of macaroni and cheese, but we were not
hungry for food. Later in the morning two church
groups, the Red Cross, and other friends came bringing
support and comfort. Looking back I believe those who
were willing to provide a service for us were most
helpful.

Of course, we take this habit of substituting food for
affection with us into our later years as well.

They had lived together for fifty four years. Many
people at the anniversary celebration commented "—
how good they look—they must really love one another." John and Mary did love one another and this
special gathering would be their last! Four days after
the meeting, John died.

Mary learned that without her partner, her life
changed dramatically. For a week or two on a regular
basis, people came by, but then the loneliness moved
in. She missed the company; no one touched her now.
Others seemed busy with their own schedules and
seldom included Mary . She told those closest to her
that she was "—wearing a path in her carpet to her
refrigerator door," and those friends noticed the weight
gain but said nothing.

When one of her girlfriends suggested that she get

involved with something so that she wouldn't be so tempted to overeat, Mary asked, "What can I do?" She was told that she could use her new car to deliver meals for the Meals-On-Wheels program. She could barely contain her excitement and was early Monday to deliver three meals—the last to an eighty one year old bachelor named Bob.

On Tuesday, when the regular driver didn't show up, Mary was called and she delivered to the same three homes, telling Bob as she left, "I'll be back tomorrow; it's my regular turn."

Bob dressed up just a bit nicer on Wednesday. As he greeted Mary at the door, he invited her to come in and "—sit awhile." She had nothing else to do so she sat across the table from Bob in his well kept kitchen. Bob pushed the food aside. Mary encouraged him to "—eat the food while it's hot—", and Bob told her "—food isn't important when I've got someone to talk to."

Mary pulled the food back, she opened it, and she ate most of it. She sat there until well after three thirty.

Many of you know the rest of the story. Now, they're living together—in sin. If they get married they would lose their social security.

Need # 3

IDENTITY.

All of us need to know that we are important people. Each one of us needs to be somebody. Every one of us **will be** somebody. In the things you do, you'll be telling me a little about who you believe that you are . You'll learn a bit about who I think you are as you see my response to what you do. Whether we're six months old, six years old, or sixty years old, whether we're actors or responders, we continually learn more about who we are and how we impact the world. When you attend to my negative, hurtful, and destructive behaviors, I learn that I'm a negative, hurtful, and destructive person. Notice me as positive, helpful, and constructive and I'll become more of each of these.

A sixteen year old kid has just bought his first car, a 1966 Mustang which is forty percent rust. He spent several hours cleaning and polishing his car, and now he drove down Main Street at twenty-five miles per hour. No one noticed. After a turn around he came back up Main Street at thirty-five miles per hour. Again no one noticed. Back at home he took the remainder of the muffler off the car, and started down Main Street at forty miles per hour—in second gear. Several young gals noticed and gave their verbal approval. After his arrest for speeding, illegal equipment, and reckless driving, he knew we had noticed. And now he has a firm idea about who he is, and he'll become even more of that. What do we catch them doing? Who do we tell them they are?

In the previous section we talked of little children demanding attention to know that they are loved. In the same act the child learns about his or her identity. Parents learn very quickly that behaviors which receive attention will be repeated. Have you ever said to a child, "I've told you a thousand times not to do that!"? Each time the child received attention for doing "that", the child, needing attention, learned to do "that" again with the same result. So, when a child performs and significant others pay attention to the behavior, the child files that information away for use at another time.

Today as he'd done many times before, a child walked through the department store with his mother. He spied a toy he'd recently seen advertised on Saturday morning television. On those previous trips he had learned that asking didn't get the toy, that begging didn't get the toy, that pouting didn't get the toy, and that withdrawing and threatening to run away didn't work. Today he'll throw a loud and magnificent tantrum. Think with me now, if mother buys the toy today, what will the child have learned? What will he try first next time? How will others see him? What has he become?

By responding to the children when the constructive and helpful sides are being displayed, we reinforce behaviors which lead to a positive identity. Children who think highly of themselves will behave in accordance with their view of self. They will start to see mistakes, accidents, failures, and shortcomings as inconsistent with their identity and will use them as learning experiences.

Here's a reminder for us all. How we respond to the behaviors of our children helps them to know who they are. Have you ever had a child spill something in a public place?

The brand new fast food restaurant was crowded. I sat alone next to a table for four only half filled. The woman about thirty sat across the diagonal from a man about the same age. Not one time did I see them interact in any way. Questions filled my mind. "Are they strangers having chosen the same table of necessity because of the crowded condition? Are they angry with one another? Are they, as some cynical voices suggest in my workshops, married to one another?" It's really none of my business I thought, but still I wondered.

In the corner of the room the door of the men's room flew open and out of that area burst two of the most energetic and beautiful five year old twin boys one could imagine. As they raced recklessly across the room they bumped people, they apologized, they laughed, they played. Upon their arrival at the table beside me, Mom and Dad came to life. I suspect with their active boys in the restroom, Mom and Dad were worried—about the condition of the restroom.

The parents had coffee and each of the boys an orange drink served in a large paper cup with a plastic cover. Whoever created that cup hasn't considered five year old children's dexterity, as they made the cup little on the bottom and big on the top. The youngster beside his mother noticed that the cover on his cup wasn't down tightly so with no thought of consequences, he placed his fingers on the edge of the cup and pushed downward. The bottom of the cup slipped easily on the ceramic table, the top of the cup fell toward the child, and instantly orange drink poured onto his lap. Mother grabbed for the napkins in the center of the table, turned toward her son, and said one word which had to contribute to his thoughts of his own worth. She said, "Whoops!"

Her response surprised me so much that I failed to see Dad leave. He returned with a cloth towel to clean the orange drink off denim jeans and the chair. The waiter, seeing the accident, set a second orange drink in front of the child. The boy thanked him for the replacement and

then noticed that the cover on this second cup wasn't down tightly. One could hear the little boy THINK. He pushed the cup across the table to his daddy and spoke with a quiet subdued voice, "Would you fix it?"

Daddy's large left hand engulfed the cup while he snapped the cover firmly into place with his right hand. Daddy winked and smiled as he pushed the cup back to the youngster.

I've asked people often to identify what the child learned and most frequently people say that he "—learned to fix the cover on the orange drink."

They are right, of course, he probably learned that. He also learned many other important things, for examples: 1) I am not what I do, and 2) I can learn from my mistakes in a safe environment, and 3) life with my family is secure and accepting. What would you have a child learn who had just spilled something?

Children who become comfortable with themselves and are clear about their roles and their worth relax enough to learn about the world they live in. They also see the best of things in their worlds. They have opportunities to practice many of the helpful and constructive skills they've learned and the response they receive perpetuates the growth. I had a chance to meet kids like this when I was a guest on the campus at the Milton Hershey School, in Hershey, Pennsylvania.

My late morning presentation to the elementary students of the Hershey school ended as the lunch hour began, and the principal asked me to join the young people at lunch. I was one of eight at our circular table. Our host, an eleven year old boy, was sitting directly across from our server, a fourth grade boy. Our host introduced all people to others present and then instructed the server to bring our food to the table. Today's lunch consisted of one bowl of tomato soup per person, a plate filled with tuna fish sandwiches, and a

carton of milk.

As we ate our food, each child had an opportunity to present his or her own ideas. For those who were reluctant to share, I asked several questions: "How did you enjoy the chapel exercise this morning?", "What did you bring for this afternoon's sharing?", "What will you do this weekend when the visitors from downtown visit the school?", and to the youngest, a child of perhaps six years, "What is your favorite pet?"

I was working especially hard to encourage one little girl whose answers had been mostly short responses to direct questions. She seemed to like the attention, and that may have been part of the reason for her being a bit shy.

My host demonstrated remarkable diplomacy for a child as he looked directly at me and said, "Dr. Kern, you can eat just as slowly as you want to; but we can't leave until you're done."

Adolescence is popularly known as the time of the "identity crisis," a time when the question, "Who am I?" occupies the center of a young person's attention. In their quest to both determine who they are and to demonstrate independence, so much a part of their lives, adolescents face many choices and this can lead to much confusion. Who are my friends to be? What will my parents think of my friends? How shall I dress? What shall I do with my spare time? Who do my parents think I am? Who do my peers think I am? Who do my teachers think I am? Who can I trust? What will I do with my life? There are questions about sex, about drugs, about religion, about college, about work, about music, about love, and about me.

I put on many masks during this time in my life. When the masks I choose get a response which I like, I adopt the mask as a part of me. I may get into a place where I don't know what is mask and what is really me.

Parents often know that the clothing chosen by their adolescents serves as a mask. Have you chosen clothes for your teenager? Have you questioned their choices?

Have they questioned your choices for them?

Those of you who have attended my workshops or
speeches know that my clothes are comfortable and
may reflect an adolescent part of me which still lives.
What grand fun I have when I ask people how they had
expected me to dress. Typical answers are these:
Formally, suit, tie, vest, or sport coat. My second
question: "What do these garments tell you about me?"
Over time I have come to prize these answers especially: An older woman in Atlanta: "It's obvious his wife
isn't with him." A young woman in Dallas: "You've had
a house fire, and haven't had time to get your wardrobe
back together yet." My clothes pretty accurately tell
people that they might expect me to be casual, relaxed,
conversational and comfortable that way.

Commencement addresses provide an avenue for
me to use clothes to make a statement. The stage is
filled with dignitaries properly dressed, but they are
not necessarily comfortably dressed. I'm almost always
comfortably dressed. If I have a coat at all, I remove it
before I begin to speak.

A farmer came forward after my address in western Minnesota with a lovely light hearted comment.
"We never go anywhere without my wife nagging me
about wearing a tie. I just hate those things, but to
keep the peace I wear them. When you got up there
today with no tie and no coat, I decided the next time
she wants me to wear a tie, I'm going to say, 'Remember that graduation speaker who—.'"

At the end of my speech in southeastern Wisconsin
a woman approached saying, "We should have known
from your informal attire that this would not be a
typical graduation speech." Raising her arms she
literally shouted, "Hooray!"

At dinner prior to a graduation address in Mi-
noqua, Wisconsin, I was eating a prime rib dinner. I
sliced off one piece of meat, lifted it about eight inches
above my plate, and that meat leaped off my fork, and
fell back into the juice on my plate. The juice spotted
my white short sleeved turtle neck shirt. I immediately looked up to see if anyone had seen my behavior.
An eighty year old woman looking right at me covered
her mouth and snickered. Then she put her finger on

her shoulders and gave me a sign which indicated I could turn my shirt around. I did that and gave my talk with my identity badly stained—up the entire back.

Clothes—Identity—one may represent the other. Parents have purchased clothing for teens only to watch them deliberately destroy the clothes, leave them at friends' houses, hang them up on the floor, or kick them underneath the bed. I've given this advice to parents of teens many times, "If you buy a garment for your child because you like the garment, buy it in your size—because you'll be wearing it if anyone does."

Finally, the attitude we hold toward ourselves forms the filters through which all other elements of our lives are considered. Believing that I'm OK helps me to see OK traits in all other people in my world.

<u>Need # 4</u>

SAFETY.

People who feel safe and secure in their worlds are positioned to give their best and also receive the most in their lives. From earliest infancy to old age we desire to be free from embarrassment, harassment, insults, bodily harm and catastrophe. In the face of these things which threaten my perception of safety, I will mobilize all of my energies to simply survive. This leaves me precious little energy for other things.

One highly visible area which demonstrates clearly how a performance can be impaired when someone doesn't feel safe exists in public speaking. Reports have been advanced which indicate that nothing provides greater fear in people than having to get in front of a group to say a few words. I have worked with scholars who have made monumental contributions to the world's knowledge storehouse who just tremble when asked to present a paper. On one occasion, a woman told me just prior to her talk, "I just hate this," and she changed from a wonderfully warm and entertaining woman into a person who read her paper in a monotone without once looking up to touch her audience with her eyes. Each time these things happen, her perceptions indicate that this is not something she does well, she will feel even less safe the next time, and her subsequent performances will become more and more unsatisfactory.

My attention has been directed to helping the children of our world to have a better place in which to live. I will continue to work toward that world where we have safer streets, safer schools, and safer homes for all people.

SAFETY ON THE STREETS—OUR NEIGHBORHOODS.

As a child I lived in a village in southeast Minnesota where the streets were safe. We were told stories of "gypsies" who would ride into town on freight trains to spirit away little children. In retrospect I believe this was my mother's way to keep us from talking to strangers and to keep us away from train cars parked near the grain elevator. Doors were seldom if ever locked, people walked outdoors late at night and children had the freedom to go all about town with little fear of danger.

Today I live in a major city where we need to be much more careful. As I sat at my desk writing these words and listening to the sound of my neighbor's lawn edger at work in his hands, I watched a young man walk up their driveway, take a bike from their garage, and ride away. The event happened so very quickly that by the time I had run out of our house and across the street to report the incident, the thief was out of sight. That theft was especially meaningful since my daughter had lost a bike only one week before. I long for the time when we won't need to lock up and guard so carefully. At times I think of the days of yesterday when the junior high school age kids gathered together on the west end of town for a game best played after sundown.

Kids from all across town gathered almost every Friday evening to play many different games including our favorite, kick the can. There were so many places to hide as the streets were not well lit. Occasionally one guy and one gal would hide away together and dream of a world in the future where they could marry and raise a family.

Sometimes we were asked to move our game to another yard, and then unsuspecting surprises awaited those who would risk an attempt to kick the can to free the "prisoners". A hole in the ground could not be seen well in the darkness and sprained ankles were prevalent. Low hanging clotheslines, just about neck high, taught many of us to run with a strange posture.

Games frequently lasted until after midnight and I now recall walking home alone. The street lights were dim and spaced far apart. The doors on the houses along the way were often open, always unlocked. I knew the people well inside those houses and they knew me. Had I needed help, it was close at hand. The streets were safe.

Frequently now when I walk on the streets after dark of many cities in our country, I remember those walks to my home. I wonder what we need to do to create safe streets once more where people won't be threatened.

SAFETY IN OUR SCHOOLS.

For children to spend energies to learn in schools, they must believe the school is a safe place for them. As I write these words I hear of still another shooting of students at a school. As much as is possible, children must know they will not be hurt or embarrassed. Then, they will be free to try new activities and enter unfamiliar territories of learning. When children begin to learn new skills or encounter new people with new techniques, they are very vulnerable. If the school environment threatens children, they'll have great difficulty growing and learning. Have you had school experiences which dramatically affected your adult life? Could you envision people carrying pain from a hurtful school experience for many years after the event?

In his recent book, Take Charge: A Guide to Feeling Good,* Wally Johnston teaches the world how to learn about the joy available when people let go of past pain and begin to take charge of their own lives. Many people labor under the pain of past experience and refuse to take that step necessary to let go of yesterday's hurts in order to gain a new measure of joy.
At the beginning of many workshops as a way to direct people toward meeting a stranger, I choose a partner and we walk through a brief encounter. I tell of two warriors on a feudal battlefield who carry shields on their left arms and weapons in their right hands as they approach one another. Each time that I have used this demonstration, my imaginary weapon of choice has been " —a short, sharp knife." Often my partner will choose something bigger, or longer, or more powerful, swords, lances, guns, or lasers. A woman in Fargo, North Dakota, won the audience' hearts when she chose "—a rusty diaper pin."
During one of our early sessions for the pastors' conference on outdoor ministries, Homer reluctantly agreed to be my partner. When he chose " —a sharp-fanged alligator" for his weapon, the entire assemblage burst into immediate and prolonged laughter. While I

* Order from: Acorn Endeavors, P.O. Box 3336, Gresham, OR. 97030

was confused at his choice, I treated Homer with the same kindness anyone deserves when in a high pressure situation. This marvelous moment would temper the rest of that session and the entire weekend experience.

I found this letter on my arrival home, and my joy was overwhelming. Consider the growth in this person as he explains his personal introspection after an early school encounter:

September 14, 1987
Mr. James L. Kern
1408 Eveningstar Road
Jelm, Wyoming 82063

The week-end of September 12, could easily have contained the most meaningful single experience in my Christian life. Thanks!

You eased aside the armor of my soul, in public, and after deftly tuning my emotional guitar, you plucked a few notes from the string labeled "cry". I did! A first since childhood. You observed and your private look said "gotcha" Homer! It was fun.

I mentioned being spanked as a first grader in front of the class and how I prepared for the next thrashing with extra clothing. The padding made it easier to hold back the tears and my fake howls made the class laugh.

That painful childhood memory and my desire to get some laughs were evaluated, unintentionally. It happened when I tried to explain why I selected an alligator for a weapon! The answer wasn't immediately apparent, but became crystal clear as the memories unfolded. Humor, that deflected ridicule and humiliation in first grade, has worked more often than not, since then, when I have been brought to the front of a group. The "alligator" was an invention to protect my ego. A traditional weapon, when set down, would

leave me vulnerable, not so with an "alligator".

I have a good life and family, many loving friends and a good job. So this resentment thing hasn't been a pitfall. But the fear of public humiliation has made me more of a private person, at times, than was proper for personal or professional growth.

New acquaintances I met on Saturday and Sunday would say, "Oh, you are Homer. Where is the alligator?" We laughed from the belly and I received positive attention. Your words about me on Saturday evening gave public acclaim. I will cherish them forever.

The fifty-year war of resentment against my first grade teacher is over. In its place is recognition of my gift of humor and the knowledge of its source. Yes, the spirit works through us.

In His name,
Homer G.

Reading aloud has never been easy for me even though I learned the skill early in my life, and I'm a very skilled reader. For this fifth grade child an oral reading experience has had a lasting effect.

He was not an especially good reader and when it came time to read out loud he was almost paralyzed. The pressure of the other fifth graders listening to him read out loud caused many physiological changes. (Some of you know them well.) On this day most of the older kids, who were given other tasks to perform while one group read aloud, had their mathematics finished and were watching the readers. He was called upon to read aloud. He was very much aware of the onlookers. His passage included this famous line from naval history, "Damn the torpedoes, full speed ahead."

Other than the slow deliberate pace he had established which allowed him to determine the correct pronunciation of the words, nothing had been unusual in his reading. Then came the line and the quotation marks indicated he should give this passage special emphasis. He saw an opportunity to "do it right" and maybe this would help him overcome past ridicule. Not only was he loud, he gave the passage proper inflection, "Damn the tadpoles, full speed ahead!"

The laughter burst initially from the eavesdroppers in the upper grade kids and eventually came from every corner of the room. There is absolutely no place for a child to hide, and the teasing became nearly

intolerable.

I recently met him on the streets of his home town, and as we approached one another I felt joyous at seeing him and I laughed. He misinterpreted my laugh as a reminder of an earlier day, and he said, "I know, tadpoles."

I wonder if even today, when this very successful man rises to speak, he thinks of that moment when he inadvertently reduced the danger to a naval fleet by mispronouncing just one word.

SAFETY IN OUR HOMES.

I'm aware that there are homes today where wives do not feel safe. There are homes where husbands do not feel safe, and I personally am most distressed when we have homes where our children do not feel safe. Stories of children having to resort to kill a parent terrify and anger me. Some of the kids who are being hurt have shared with me and with others the unthinkable things adults do to them. Many of these kids show up in hospitals, some in police stations, and a few in morgues. But what can we do about the unknown number of children who are being abused, neglected, or hurt day after day with no help in sight? The thoughts of these kids prompts me to assure them whenever I can, that I will always be their friend, that I will be available to them, and that I'll not turn them away. In cooperation with school officials, I know I've been able to help some. There are many, many more needing help.

I've worked long and hard to create a safe place for each of my own six children. Still I could fill several chapters with stories of my shortcomings and failures. On one occasion I did things right and rejoice in the effect it's had on my son Chris in his relationship with his father.

When Chris was sixteen years old, he fell in love for the very first time. Whenever Susie was near him, his senses went to zero; he couldn't hear, he couldn't see, he couldn't smell. On this January night in southern Minnesota, the temperature dropped to nineteen degrees below zero.

Chris received permission to use my pick-up truck on this frigid night and from seven in the evening until she would get off work, he drove—he called it "cruised"—back and forth on third street. His friend, Scott, cruised with him and together they arrived to pick her up at the end of her shift at the pizza palace. She slid into the truck, sat right up next to him and his senses shorted out. They decided that they would drive to LaCrosse, Wisconsin, about twenty-six miles away to get a Happy Joe's Pizza. (Now there's a Happy Joe's Pizza place in Winona, it's open, and to understand why they're driving to LaCrosse—well you'd have to be sixteen again.)

Driving the truck in this zombie-like state, he was unable to notice the light on the dashboard that says "Oil" behind it burning brightly; he didn't hear the loud clicking sound the engine began to make; and he didn't smell the odor which seeped into the cab area through the firewall. All of these would be signals to most people that there's a problem under the hood. He

turned the radio louder, and they continued on eastward toward Wisconsin.

Approximately four miles upstream from that river city, there's a twenty-four hour service station tucked away in the bluffs. Near that station, Scott likely noticed the problems with the truck. He drove into the station parking area and turned the engine off. Many of you know that this engine will never run again, as inside every cylinder there is a piston securely welded.

Chris spoke to his friends saying, "We'll have to call my dad."

Scott didn't hesitate at all hearing that, "Oh, God, we can't do that." What does this say about the amount of safety and security Scott experiences with his father?

Chris called—COLLECT—and the ringing phone awakened me after forty minutes of sound sleep. His first words were, "Guess what, Dad!"

"Guessing games in the middle of the night, son? What is it?"

"Well, Dad, I think I've run your pick-up out of oil."

Do any of you know what our first response will be when we hear words like that? I was proud of myself when I said, "Where are you?"

"I'm in that station just above LaCrosse, Wisconsin."

"I'll be right there." I placed the receiver down and walked into the bedroom. I was just seething with anger as I spoke, "He's run the pick-up out of oil."

"Remember, he'll need a safe place now."

I thought to myself, I'll fix a safe place for him all right. I dressed and entered our small car. It started despite the temperature and I started to drive toward LaCrosse rehearsing all the things I wouldn't say. As I pulled into the station, Sue and Scott ran toward the car. Chris walked very slowly. He began to get into the car and I asked, "Have you forgotten something you'll be needing?" He'd forgotten his watch so he walked ever so slowly back to get it. This time he got into the car, fastened his belt, turned to his friends in the back seat of the car and said, "See, I told you he wouldn't be mad at me!"

I had many things I wanted to share as we drove toward Winona, but it's hard to speak with your heart crowded into your throat like that. I turned the radio up louder.

We stopped at Sue's house and she left, "Good night, Sue." We stopped at Scott's house and he left, "Good night, Scott."

Chris had closed the door now and he looked right into my heart as he shared, "Dad, I was so proud of you tonight."

I crawled back into bed next to a warm body. We heard him rustling around in his room, and then came a knock on the door. Chris came in with a small jar filled with cash. He stated his case so well, "Dad, the last engine you bought cost two hundred fifty dollars. I only have one hundred twenty three, but I'll help you put it in."

Many of you know it's a joy to work on a pick-up with your son. The truck would eventually become his (partly since he already owned half the engine), he would go on to become a wonderful young man who knows where to find safe places—even when it appears he's made a big mistake.

BUILD THE FORT...TODAY!

Part III

Pathways to Pain

BUILD THE FORT...TODAY!

Our health and well being depends upon our success in fulfilling our needs as outlined in the previous section. Our bodies require rest, food, protection from elements and sexual gratification. We function best with the knowledge that we are loved, we are important, and we are safe. Joy comes to those people who have those four needs met and who are willing to work hard toward acquiring joy. For those people who do not feel loved, important, and safe, who aren't fed and protected or who don't put forth the energy to have joy, pain will be a ready companion.

In this section I'll be presenting four of the ways people can get pain in their lives. My goal in the discussion will be to give you insights which would position you to be helpful to another. Good friends to people in pain play an important role in the healing process. I recommend professional help for people who seem to be forever hurting, but you can become an invaluable resource with these insights into the pain we all know.

I will share with you four pathways to the acquisition of pain in your life: 1) the pain which grows from a loss, 2) the pain we choose, 3) the pain of failure, and 4) the pain we experience when we live in unequal psychological relationships. I'll discuss each of these in a separate section which may lead you to believe that they operate alone and are unrelated one to another. Nothing could be further from the truth. These four pathways work together so closely that seldom does a person experience just one. As you read about someone's choosing pain, be aware that this person may well be involved as a loser in at least one relationship, may be in the midst of failure, and probably knows the despair of loss.

Should you desire to help someone who's hurting, you may want to consider the commitment you'll need to make in order to be effective. A hit and run approach will do more harm than good. If I position myself as a helper to someone and then leave for some reason, this person will experience an unnecessary loss or could see the failure of the relationship to be her/his responsibility.

Your commitment as a sincere helper may not demand a long expenditure of time for you to be effective. Under the principle of change I suggested that one person cannot change another. Here I will discuss another kind of problem which we may create if we believe we can solve problems for another. Wally Johnston wrote a book to encourage people to take charge of their own lives in order to feel good. In his work, Wally includes a section entitled, "Quick Fixes for Minor Snags" which you might find helpful. In a relatively short time we may provide insights for growth, remove blocks which prevent progress, or comfort someone by giving our support. We can work together to reduce the pain people endure.

Pathway # 1

EXPERIENCING LOSS.

During a given period of time we all experience losses. We've lost possessions, pets, friends, relationships, jobs, opportunities, loved ones, and the list could go on for pages. The feelings which accompany these losses vary in intensity, but probably do not vary a great deal in type. Simply stated, we hurt when we experience most losses. (One exception, of course, would be the loss of weight which we've worked to accomplish) To be your helper I would use the word "hurt" in a response to that hurting person. Many people have difficulty in saying the word which best describes their own feeling or position. Heavy people seldom use the word "fat", divorced people frequently avoid the word "divorced", and people who hurt need for us to say what they're feeling. Helpers learn to look at the world through the eyes of another and report what they see, and also report how the other must feel.

Try your helping skills in these situations. When I was fourteen years old my mother died very suddenly as she returned home from the grocery store. You might look out through my eyes and report, "It hurts so much when you lose your mother." In 1978 our house burned and we lost many valuable possessions in addition to the house. Once again you can report the feelings of any family member as you say, "You have to hurt when you see your valuable things in ashes."

You don't need to share your experiences or your feelings. The words, "I know how you must feel because my mother died when I was young," may not help me now. If you know how I feel, then report what I might be feeling.

You won't be able to solve my problem. Over the years children have experienced hurt and emptiness when a favorite pet dies or is killed. People who genuinely want to be helpful by solving the child's problem have said "Don't worry, honey, we'll get you another one." You would never think of saying that to a widow, would you?

You can be helpful to anyone who has experienced a loss by doing three things. 1) In my hurt I would appreciate someone who UNDERSTANDS how I feel who does not say, "I understand how you feel." If you understand how I feel, then say the words which describe how you think I feel. If you are absolutely wrong, I'll correct you, and as I talk you'll have a clearer understanding, and I'll gain insights as well. If you're right on target, I'll know that you do understand. 2) When I'm hurting, I want to be with someone who CARES for me. In the previous section I discussed showing someone we care to meet our own need for affection. These same three techniques work here. Paying attention, touching, and listening to hurting people demonstrate our caring for them. 3) Be PRESENT with me. When people experience their grief, they receive much support and strength from caring people who are willing to be present. As a helper you may feel awkward, uncomfortable, or miserable in the presence of someone who's grieving. You may find it easier to put your discomfort aside as you realize how very helpful you can be.

So often when people have experienced pain-filled losses they find themselves facing an immediate second loss, the loss of the friends who would support them and help them through this most hurtful time. How often have we all heard people say these or similar things? 1) "I just wouldn't know what to say," 2) "I just wouldn't be able to avoid crying myself," 3) "I thought he/she would like to have some time alone." Consider for a moment the hurt and continuous pain of the people briefly described in the following paragraphs.

"Isn't it enough that I've lost my son? Do I have to lose my friends, too?" The young teacher who spoke these words had called home to encourage his wife to make preparations for a quick trip into town. She wasn't strong enough to pull the wagon to the Jeep so when he got home he was in a big hurry. He pulled the wagon to the Jeep, and attached it. He scrambled into the driver's seat as his wife hurried into the rider's place. Both of them assumed that their three year old boy would be playing in the back of the vehicle, "— that's where he always was," he explained. He started the engine and drove ahead such a short distance. How could he have known that his little boy had crawled under the car perhaps to help a smaller animal?

Mom and Dad drive quickly with the boy to the hospital miles away only to hear these saddest of all words, "He's been dead for about an hour." The ride home had to seem very long. He spoke about the emptiness and the helplessness and about the silence in the house especially at night when it was so hard to sleep.

Finding the appropriate words is not at all easy. I remembered that we must speak the words which describe the feelings of the bereaved for them, the words which they cannot say at this moment. I ventured these, "Is that the hurt now?"

"No, our pastor has been very helpful and we've pretty well accepted his death. The hurt now is this: I walk into this building in the morning and people are gathered in small groups just talking. If I walk into the group, people often turn and walk away."

Is it possible that they don't know what to say? Is it possible they won't be able to handle their own fears and sorrows if they speak with him at this time of intense need for friends nearby?

* * * * * *

"I can empty the entire vestibule of the church just by mentioning my son's name." The motorcycle accident which claimed her son's life was particularly hard for her since she had never liked motorcycles, thought they were much too dangerous, and had vigorously argued against his having one. She became worried that her need to talk about the accident coupled with her friends' reluctance or fears would drive them forever apart.

* * * * * *

"The sky's so big that no two planes would ever collide, but they did collide and he's gone." Being alone when you believe you need to talk to someone isn't very comfortable for a father who has just lost a talented son who flew fighter planes for the United States Air Force. "We always set a place for him at meal time and remember him especially during the holidays."

* * * * * *

"We did everything we could for Mom—we did everything we could." He needs to tell the story over and over again.

We learned of her death as Paul was reading the paper when he noticed the announcement of the funeral of his wife. They were both very close to our family and we wanted to be present at the funeral. He seemed so far away from us at the funeral home and at the gravesite. I knew his heart would be breaking even as he spent time with his family and friends. My schedule demanded that I get on the road again.

When I returned from that trip, I rode my motorcycle to his place down the river a bit and we had a chance to talk about his loss. Over and over again he spoke the words, "We did everything we could for Mom—."

I'm sure he did everything that could be done for her. My listening to him say it again and again will help him to know that.

* * * * * *

The administrative team members had worked hard to discover unique ways to position themselves to be most helpful to those who had experienced painful losses. Two people became intensely aware of their own pain during the discussion and had shared that they had each in the very recent past lost two children. Many agreed that the loss of a child might be the greatest loss one would ever need to experience. This awareness brought her to the front of the group where she shared her thoughts with the group: "We all live our lives," she started, "believing that we will outlive our parents. We experience hurt when our mothers and fathers die, but somehow we knew we would be here after they were gone. We don't live our lives believing we're going to outlive our children. So, if our children should die, we experience not only the tremendous hurt, but also the shock which accompanies their unexpected death.

"When our parents die, we lose a bit of yesterday. When our children die, we lose a good bit of tomorrow."

124

Dr. Elisabeth Kubler-Ross has accomplished much in
helping people who are bereaved. In her book, <u>On Death
and Dying,</u> she presents five stages through which
people might move as they grieve a loss or anticipate
their death or the death of another. Knowledge of the
stages may give us the insights necessary to express the
understanding we've discussed. Read the book to learn
how people handle their 1) denial, 2) anger, 3) bargaining, 4) depression, and finally 5) acceptance of their
losses.

These five stages have a tremendously universal
application. I've even lost things which were quite incon-
sequential and have experienced these stages. I think
about the loss of a fish, a golf ball, or a small coin in a
vending machine. I learned of graduate students who
were asked to write short narratives designed to be so
common and simple that all people could relate to them
and remember the stages. I've enjoyed these two papers
a good deal.

"Have you ever lost a contact lens?" the paper begins.
I could have filled in the rest as I remembered Denise's
reaction to losing one of her lenses. In her denial stage

she will come to me, stretch her eye open widely, and say, "It must be in there somewhere, can you see it?" At the anger level she says things which can't be printed here. In her bargaining stage you might hear her say, "Oh, God, if I could just find it this time, I'll never again rinse it without pushing the plunger down." Depression fills her life until that time she calls to get a replacement.

The other paper started with a statement, "I go through all five stages every morning when my alarm clock rings." Use your own experience to work through the stages.

I'm one who believes that the loss of a child would be the most intense and severe loss for anyone to encounter. The hurt of losing my 'tomorrows' with a child would be extremely painful. This letter came to my home.

Mr. Jim Kern
15114 Heimer
San Antonio, TX 78232

Dear Jim,

We met at the A.A.S.P.A. conference in San Diego on October 19, 1987. After your presentation, I told you the story of our son's death. You asked me to write my story and send it to you. Several others have made the same request, but you were the first to acknowledge that it would be hard to do so. You were right.

I want to begin with some brief background information. On October 20, 1967, I started my day, as I often did then, by telephoning my mother. I was 24, married to an elementary school teacher, and had a 17 month old son, Mark. My parents were expected to stop by our apartment that evening. Plans were made, and I said good-bye. At approximately 3:00 PM, my father and younger sister were at my door telling me that my mother had died suddenly earlier that day. This was my first experience with death. I damned God and turned from him. Having been raised a Catholic and having attended parochial schools, this was a major step for me. I also "packed my mother off on a long trip" and refused to acknowledge her death.

On December 20th, exactly two months later, I walked by 19 month old Mark's crib and found that he had gone into convulsions. He was a very sick child. He convulsed five more times that day as I alone stayed with him at the hospital. The last convulsion brought the "code blue" call, and I was forced to leave his room. A nurse coming out of his room was overheard saying, "I don't think he will live." I went off by myself and made my peace with God by finally accepting my mother's death. I asked God to give my baby back to me to raise for a few years, and then, if he needed him, to take him after He had allowed us to watch him grow. The next morning, Mark was standing in his hospital crib with a big welcome for me. None of his doctors were sure about what had happened, but I knew. The day Mark came home from the hospital, we learned that our son Paul would be born in August, 1968.

The next 17 years were full and happy. We had a strong family unit. Charlie, my husband, became an elementary school principal, and I started working as a kindergarten teacher's aide when Paul entered first grade. We spent Saturdays on the ball fields. During the boys' high school years, we spent time on the band bus chaperoning for "away" ball games and band competitions. Time flew by. Life was good. We attended a nearby Episcopal church, and both boys rose to the rank of senior acolyte and became leaders in the youth group.

Sunday, August 4, 1985 was Paul's 17th birthday. He was very excited about his upcoming senior year in high school. Shortly after Paul's birthday, my sister, Pam, made a rare and welcomed visit from her home in California. She wanted to see the nephews she hadn't seen in about five years. She knew they were growing up. Pam left and went to Florida to visit our father who was dying of cancer. Charlie and Mark busied themselves packing and preparing to return Mark to North Carolina for his second year of college.

When the house was once again quiet, Paul came to me and asked, "Now that everybody is out of here, I want to go to the grocery store with you and get some of the things I like." We got up Saturday morning and

went to an auto shop. He showed me the things he
wanted for the car that he had once shared with Mark,
but was now his own. He bought a couple of things, and
we went off to the grocery store. He was in a silly mood.
We went up and down every aisle. He put things we
had never had before in the cart. "Try it, we may like
it." When we got back home, I spent some time outside
as he worked on "his" car. Charlie came home that
afternoon.

Paul was scheduled to serve as acolyte at the 9:30
AM service at church Sunday morning. We were awake
as he was getting ready. He was playing a Billy Joel
tape with the song, "Only the Good Die Young." After
he left for church, and we were getting dressed, Charlie
started humming the same tune. I asked him to please
stop as it was a terrible thought.

I was eating lunch at approximately 12:30 that
afternoon. Charlie had gone to his school to get some
last-minute things done because the teachers were to
report the next day to start a new school year. It was
raining hard outside — the fringes of a hurricane. The
doorbell rang. A very nervous policeman in a yellow
raincoat was standing on the porch. He asked if I was
alone, which I was. I asked to see his I.D. and stepped
out to look for his car. He told me straight out that
Paul had been killed at approximately 10:30 AM on one
of the main roads in the rain. I had known he was
meeting a friend after church at McDonald's so I had
not worried when he didn't come right home. He never
made it to McDonald's. He was alone in his car. No one
in the other car was hurt. Paul had died.

The weeks that followed were filled with unbeliev-
able love and support from our community. Because we
live in a relatively transient suburb of Washington,
D.C., this was unexpected. There were 20 accidents
that Sunday, August 18, 1985, because of the heavy
rain. Paul's was the only death. When the high school
band director came to visit one evening, he said it was
too bad Paul had not had his senior year. For some
reason I said without even thinking, "God had wanted
Paul as a child. A year later, he would have been a
man." I remembered that night in December, 1967,
when I had asked God to let me raise my baby then
take him if he needed him . . . . I had always thought it

would be Mark, not the unborn child I was then carrying.

We still miss Paul greatly. The pain is still in my chest, but we have moved on with our lives. We still have a strong support group at our church and are thankful that we have become closer to God and not drifted away.

In case you forgot the purpose of my coming up to you that day, it was not to relay my religious experience, but to tell you that there are some parents out there who do take the time to be with their kids and love every minute of it. Nobody ever knows what tomorrow might bring — so do it today.

Sincerely,

Eileen R.

To summarize this section let me suggest that helpers go to people who have experienced loss with love and support, putting their own needs aside for a time so their full attention goes to the other. We need to support these hurting people.

Pathway # 2

CHOOSING PAIN.

I'm quite sure that every person at sometime in his or her life has chosen to be sick or disabled, often to avoid an uncomfortable or intolerable life situation. Often people commit themselves to work or life situations which carry huge responsibility with little reward. One way out is to choose some illness or disability. With your checking account balance near zero and your loan payments overdue, you resist going to the bank to talk with someone. Your mind can make your body sick. For me, dental appointments can cause me to choose disability.

Children learn very early the possibilities of choosing illness to avoid responsibility. On one particular morning a youngster wants to stay home so he will over-dramatize his 'sickness' for his mother's attention. After a cursory examination (which often includes placing her palm on his forehead), Mother fixes a place for him on the couch, brings the nicest pillow in the house and fluffs it for him, covers him with a blanket which smells of mothballs, turns on the television, changes the channel on command, brings a TV tray with orange juice and lemonade, calls Grandma and she's coming with a dollar. Children learn the lesson in one trial—Mom serves me, helps me, and gives me extra attention whenever I tell her I'm not feeling well. The child will get sick whenever he sees the need for these things.

Mothers, when you suspect that the child chooses or feigns illness, you might want to remember this line, "If you're not feeling well, you'll need rest in a dark quiet place." If the consequences of being sick are less pleasant than the consequences of facing responsibility, the child will not choose illness.

What causes people to allow their children to feign illness to avoid responsibility? We can better understand the condition as we consider the relationship between our hearts (our feelings) and our heads (our thoughts). Some of us have a:

SOFT HEART and a SOFT HEAD. If you recognize in yourself a soft heart, you may want to ask if your heart has ever made your head soft. Finding yourself here indicates that you have a tendency to serve others so well and so much that they won't need to do things for themselves. Your "mothering" part may become a "smothering" part. You have the traits often associated with the "enabler" role.

HARD HEAD and a HARD HEART. If you recognize these characteristics, has your head ever made your heart hard? I've teased for years saying that this combination will allow you to go into administration, and I'm not sure people hear me add right afterward, "—and you'll fail miserably." Top level administrators learn quickly the disadvantages of this uncaring approach to subordinates.

HARD HEAD and a SOFT HEART. Once people discover the distinct advantages of letting their heads do their thinking and their hearts do their feeling, of letting their thoughts be hard while there is compassion in their hearts, the quality of their relationships improve. Parents will be more effective in raising children when they show much love and compassion (soft heart) while they expect and maintain high standards and clearly state the limits (hard head). Healing professionals perform best with a high level of expertise and a willingness to use their skills in combination with a compassionate bedside manner. Enablers escape the continuing pain of abuse and heartbreak once they change their thinking from serving and protecting their spouse to confronting. Administrators faced with unpleasant encounters with employees will be most effective when they demonstrate a caring nature as they deliver even the harshest information.

Hurtful events in our lives teach us to avoid similar conditions in our future. When the hurtful event occurs in the life of a young person and parents over-react, the result may become a life long avoidance behavior. My daughter Carrie still avoids situations which require mathematics ability.

> Her sparkle, her undying enthusiasm, and her very competitive nature allowed Carrie, a tenth grader, to excel in most activities; however, she consistently withdrew from experiences with mathematics and number activities. I suspected her trouble grew from an earlier incident in her education. As soon as I became aware of the difficulty I asked Carrie to meet with a counselor, we arranged for a battery of tests to be given, she spoke with a hypnotist, I checked into getting a tutor and we made no progress. Then I did what my dad, without the benefit of all that "book

learning" would have done in the first place, I asked Carrie, "Why do you not like mathematics?"

"I think it started when I was in third grade," she told me, and my mind went back to an event several years ago.

The third graders were learning to add two digit numbers. On her practice sheet Carrie completed nineteen out of twenty problems incorrectly. With no apparent fear at all she showed me her paper containing nineteen check marks and a large red "F" in the upper left hand corner. I was surprised.

With a desire to surprise her while assuring her that her relationship with her daddy was safe and secure, I asked, "How did you happen to get that first one right?"

"That one was the example we did together in class."

"Would you tell me how you did that problem in class?" She demonstrated creativity, but very little evidence that she had paid attention in class during the presentation of the example. The problem was: 57 + 53 = _____. Carrie had marked her answer, 110, on the blank.

I asked her to show me how she got the answer, and Carrie talked through her solution, "Dad, five and five is ten. You put the one down here and you carry the zero. Zero and seven and three is ten."

When her answer matched the answer the class had reached, she had no reason to question her process. She bolted ahead without further attention to her teacher and classmates responding in part to a lesson she'd learned from her competitive father about being Number One. She was the first person done and she had some very creative answers.

In just a few moments of "unlearning" and "re-learning", Carrie discovered that the skill used in reading is not appropriate for doing addition. She was comfortable with her new learning and with her world.

If I had felt that comfortable, I would not have gone to school to confront Carrie's teacher. I remember being quite harsh and almost nasty to the teacher who had graded Carrie's paper this way.

Back home I recounted the events of the confrontation and in her mind, Carrie envisioned a hurtful encounter between her daddy (whom she loved) and her teacher (whom she loved) over mathematics. She knew that one of these three things would be easy to resist and to dislike, and even today Carrie struggles with and avoids mathematics and number activities.

For the longest time blinded by my hurt, I believed her teacher was at fault for Carrie's resistance. I suspect now that the teacher was a tired teacher and was likely unaware that this child was having any problem at all. Teachers get tired of kids who bolt ahead without listening to directions. Teachers get tired of "expert" parents too willing to judge and unwilling to be helpful. Teachers get tired of increased expectations on them with little if any reward forthcoming. Have you thanked a teacher lately?

So we can choose to be in pain to avoid responsibility and to avoid disappointing or hurtful experiences. We can become disabled to the point of complete withdrawal from life, and getting sick or choosing to be disabled by choice may be a way to control or to hurt others. Arnie came to me at the end of an especially hard day and told me that he had understood this business of choosing pain first hand.

He had big tears in the corners of his eyes as he approached. In his eighty-seven years he had seen and experienced many changes in society both in his professional life as an accomplished accountant and also in his personal life as a husband and father. "You've told the story of my wife today," he confided. "Twenty years ago this woman went to bed. For twenty years I've had to do everything for her." His anger, his helplessness, and his hurt seeped into both his verbal and non-verbal messages. "She won't even get up to go to the bathroom, still she sometimes gets up when her family comes to visit."

"Have you taken her to a doctor?"

His eyes flashed and he spoke more rapidly. "I did take her to her doctor. He gave her a complete physical examination and told both of us that he could find nothing wrong with her at all." That's strange, I thought, that there wouldn't be anything wrong. He continued, "Then in the car on the way home she said, 'I don't ever want to see that doctor again.'" The doctor had apparently told her a truth she wasn't ready or willing to accept. Then, by denying his word she could cling to her choice for the use of her life, that is to choose to be disabled so that people would need to continue to be with her and to serve her.

He walked away with tears in his eyes.

During that entire evening the sight of him walking away after having received so little help from me filled my mind. He had said that she went to bed twenty years ago. He would have been sixty-seven and I would guess she was about the same age. I wondered about the possibility that the problem had its roots in his retirement. A couple of calls and several questions allowed me to gather information to complete the puzzle, to understand the rest of the story and to check on my guess about her motivation.

He was sixty-five when he gave the business formally to his only son. His wife looked into her tomorrows with dreams of traveling especially into warm climates during the winter months which had filled her life for as long as she could remember. Over these many years, he had been especially busy from the first of the year until April fifteenth, and now at last they could visit the Carribbean and the southland. Since he had always been so busy and closely identified with the business, he very likely suspected that retirement would present problems.

For two weeks he moped about and in general, was not a happy person away from his work. When his son called requesting a day or two of his expert counsel, he felt an immediate surge of exhileration. We will need you only for a couple of days his son had said. Two days at work became a week at work; the week became two weeks, and he was happy to be needed again.

She began at first to ask about the travel plans. "Later," she was told, "after we get these accounts straightened out."

Over time she became convinced that he was so looking forward to working each day that her requests would continue to be ignored. Before long her interrogations resembled nagging comments. He escaped the nagging by going to work and a pattern was quickly established.

After two years she chose a strategy to keep him home forever, she would be sick and disabled. She went to bed, she needed him at home now. If he were to leave her, she'd become worse. He chose to stay home to serve her, and before very long, both were trapped in their choices and neither was able to realize the potential happiness and adventure which might have filled their later years.

This ability to choose to be sick allows us all to check out of the mainstream of life on demand. In recent years I've observed the development of a condition which anyone can choose to avoid further responsibility. It's called "Burn out." I laughed many times at the suggestion that we shouldn't allow people to burn out unless they can provide proof that they were at least once on fire.

I believe that people who burn out have relinquished some important personal responsibility. When people allow responsibilities to grow so large while their personal reservoir of personal power is diminished, they burn out. When one's personal expenses exceed their income, a person will need to make some hard choices. The same balance must be achieved in our lives. Burn out candidates must increase that power reservoir or reduce their responsibilities.

We learned to support and comfort those who suffer losses. We must learn to treat those who choose pain much differently. To support and comfort them, will bring us into the problem as well.

Just one last thought here: If you can use your mind to make your body sick, you can also use your mind to keep your body well.

Pathway # 3

FAILURE.

Pain comes to people who experience failure. For many of us things like mistakes, accidents, and short-comings are perceived as failure, and we respond in different ways partly because we have such varied backgrounds. When our backgrounds are predominantly filled with successes, we tend to deny the failures as "Behaviors-Not-Like-Me" and we point to our success record. We live with many who have failed so frequently that they no longer think of themselves as human beings who have failed. Instead they begin to think of themselves as "Failures". Teachers work diligently to create opportunities for success among these people. Just as we deny our failures, these people tend to deny their successes. They describe successes as the same way we describe failure, as "Behaviors-Not-Like-Me."

This discussion will focus on ways to be helpful to these Failures. I'm confident these people can be helped. I get nervous thinking about the consequences of not helping them. As you read of suggestions for working with these extreme failures, I trust you'll gain insights into your own mistakes or shortcomings as well.

To provide for us a model to use in discussing the consequences of failure, let me share a relatively small mistake I made years ago.

Paul must have been nearly eight years old when he asked to have the woodwork in his room painted. He had decided that black woodwork would properly accent a room with white and red wall paper. His requests were met time and again with his dad saying, "Later." Persistance is a quality present in abundance in this age group child. He asked frequently and in many different ways. The answer didn't change.

His mother would be away for this evening, my schedule was open, so the plans were made to paint the woodwork after our evening meal. Paul could hardly wait, he was so excited.

In preparation for painting we opened a small can of black enamel in the kitchen. We stirred it well and mixed it to exactly the right consistency. Then we started up the stairs to do the work. I was first, Paul was behind me and Pam was behind Paul. The carpet on our stairway was beige.

We were very near the top of the stairs when I FAILED. I stumbled and spilled a cup or more of that black enamel onto the carpet. I'd be embarrassed to tell you what I said. Paul said, "Well, Dad, you're smarter now!"

"Don't use that counselor crap on me," I fumed.
What will we do now?"

Pam wanting to be helpful stated matter of factly,
"We could wipe it up." Have you tried to wipe black
paint off a light colored carpet? Where at first we had a
relatively manageable and small circle of paint, we now
had a large unmanageable circle. With a sparkle
dancing in his eyes, Paul informed us that we could
paint the whole carpet.

GUILT feelings rose up in me and I began to plan a
way to hide the results of my accident. My instructions
seemed clear: "Pam, why don't you go to the garage to
find a small piece of rug or carpet? We'll cover it and
maybe no one will notice it."

I was sure that my plan to hide the spill was
woefully inadequate. I was aware of a growing feeling
of FEAR—fear that their mother would learn who had
spilled the paint there. Throughout the evening I
conversed with the children helping them to understand our plan, to tell mother nothing of the spill.

When their mom came home at eleven, Pam met
her at the door and said, "Guess what Dad did!" Now I
was consumed with my next feeling: ANGER!! In fact, I
was angry with myself, but as I've done so frequently, I
chose as the target of my anger a child, a little girl who
was close by who had just narcked.

Pam needed to feel safe, so she went to her room.
Paul knew he was next, so he went to his room. Their
mother knew they needed affection, so she went up to
be with them, and I was alone with two St. Bernard
dogs. That's LONELINESS!! I realize now that I had
chosen all of these negative feelings, GUILT, FEAR,
ANGER, and LONELINESS, instead of simply admit-
ting I had spilled the paint and owned the mistake. The
paint remained on the carpet.

The narrative reveals that after I failed to own up to
my mistake, I brought into my life feelings of guilt, fear,
anger and loneliness. This model depicts how this process worked in this story:

PATHWAYS OF PAIN
THE FAILURE FUNNEL

Unrealistic
Expectations

Problems   Dilemmas

Misunderstanding   Accidents

Helping Skills
to Reduce
Pressure

► Give Information

FAILURE

► Provide Assurance

GUILT

► Express Love (eg. hug)

FEAR

► Develop Outlets

ANGER

LONELY ► Be a Friend

Pressure Builds

Energy stemming from life experiences like accidents, misunderstandings, and unrealistic perceptions
pours into the top of this hypothetical funnel of failure.
As the energy moves downward between the walls of the
funnel, both speed and pressure will be increased. The
bottom of the funnel represents that point where this
person touches the world. Just as a tornado destroys the
world it touches, this psychological tornado destroys
everything in its path. We have responded by doing a
number of things which cause more energy to flow into
the top. We punish, we label, and we imprison these
people. This results in more pressure, more speed, and
more destruction.

What could be done instead? I'm convinced that
helpers reaching into the funnel at the highest possible
levels will offer pressure releases. We can then subvert

the process by creating an upward flow of energy moving from bottom to top resulting in less pressure, less speed, and less destruction.

At each level a special skill or set of skills can be used to offer assistance to the Failure. Anyone can help to create success where once only failure existed.

FAILURE

Before my guilt engulfs me, I need new and better information. Suppose for just a moment that we could teach kids to respond to mistakes and accidents as if they were nothing more than learning experiences. They would learn very early in their lives to ask, "What can I learn from this?" One day people everywhere will know that making mistakes gives us a chance to grow to become "smarter now."

Mistakes and accidents tend to teach us valuable lessons if we remain open to those learnings. Wally Johnston recommends that we assume an attitude toward life expecting that the world is our classroom and that painful situations are mini-lessons. (Some of them are maxi-lessons.) If this be true, we no longer need respond to mishaps with feelings of despair, regret, and unhappiness with ourselves. Each one of us might raise our arms and raise our eyes and say with enthusiasm, "Well, good. I'm smarter now!"

Recall for just a minute in the midst of this serious discussion on mistakes and accidents that cold night when you went to bed early without your normal routine. It's three in the morning now; you've tossed and turned; you haven't shut an eye and you know a long cold walk to the bathroom is inevitable. You'll crawl out of bed on your side, you'll leave the lights off so as not to disturb others and you'll walk quickly because it's cold in here.

Picture your foot for only a moment: A heavy object

on the end of your leg with fragile toes out in front.

As you walk quickly through the pitch black room your toes will find the leg of your bed. Do you remember what you said at that moment? Do you remember raising your arms and eyes and saying, "Well, good. I'm smarter now."

At times in our educational institutions we deprive youngsters of the opportunity to learn from their mistakes and sometimes deliver tremendous and lasting pain to them. For years I have believed that the high school coaches can be the finest educators in the school since they establish unique relationships with many kids. This isn't always the case as you'll see.

High school basketball teams play before large crowds, and often the fans have their knees directly into the backs of the players and coaches. This arrangement allows some in the crowd to hear what coaches say to young participants and in this process provides the coach an excellent opportunity to be a superior educator who recognizes that information will help all of us overcome shortcomings, mistakes and failure. On some occasions the information transmitted will only make the condition of failure more difficult for the participant.

He was an excellent shooter as well as an excellent student. Many described this young perfectionist as high strung and nervous, like his mother. He won a starting position on the high school varsity as a very young person, and his pride and tension surfaced often in the preparation time before the first game. His parents, two sets of grandparents, and a favorite aunt and uncle would attend the game. "We'll be right behind your bench a few rows up," he was told as he left home.

The opening tip came into his hands. He dribbled forward as he'd been instructed. He heard the voice of his coach above all other sounds, "Get the ball over to the wing." He turned and in one motion released the ball toward the exact spot where the forward had been standing. The ball sailed into the crowd. Now the coach shouted even louder than before, "Just relax! Settle down!" Try as he might, he found it nearly impossible to do either.

The opponents shot an air ball which fell into his teammate's hands, the outlet pass came to him, and he started dribbling up the floor. The messages from the coach were inaudible. He turned to hear what the coach was shouting and the ball slipped away. The opponents retrieved the loose ball and now, sounds of disappointment from the rooters could not drown out the profanity and the expressed anger of the coach. He could not relax enough to shake off the jitters, the information he received was not helpful, and the pressures grew.

A very short time later the young man stepped to the free throw line to break the zero-zero score. He wanted to ignore the tension and the messages from the bench. He shot the ball and missed everything—the net, the rim, the backboard.

His peripheral vision alerted him to the activity on the bench, his substitute reported to the scorer, and he would need to leave the floor. He tried to avert his eyes so he wouldn't need to see the obvious hurt and disappointment in the faces of his family members. He sat as far from the coach as was possible.

When he returned to action, the game was pretty well decided in favor of the visitors team. He had failed.

Had the coach only relaxed enough to teach this young man to learn from his every mistake everyone would win. The boy would not have suffered the humiliation and the fans observing would realize that mistakes provide opportunities.

GUILT

Guilt causes me to want to hide, just as it did Adam and Eve in one classic story of failure. Politicians and television evangelists in the last half of the twentieth century have experienced the desire to hide as well. We can be helpful to guilt-ridden people by separating the person from the behavior. Assuring them- "You're OK when your behavior is Not OK"-allows failing people to come out of hiding to discuss the failure.

Everything about her seemed to fit the stereotype of the elementary school principal depicted in a 1950's motion picture about education in the forties. She spoke of her disgust with the "filthy magazines and films", of her lack of understanding of these "—new ideas in education" and of people's impatience in general, "—where are they going in such a hurry?" Her old-fashioned views amused me and her genuine caring flowed in many directions. She spoke of the joy that filled her school as people from the senior center came to read to her little children and then eat lunch in the school with her kids. "Why," she said pointing to an older scruffy looking gentleman, "he was here one half hour before the kids came today."

The seven year old boy bounded down the stairway to our left looking downward at the steps to avoid a fall. He turned left at floor level and was just a bit short of full speed when he noticed her. His braking system functioned well.

Sixty three years of aging didn't prevent her from going to her knees, embracing the little speedster, and reminding him gently but firmly, "You know I love you, Jason; I just can't stand running."

FEAR

When we experience increasing fear, the number of choices available to us is limited until eventually the fear can paralyze us. The antidote for that paralytic process lies in someone expressing genuine love for us. For many years people have learned that perfect love pushes out fear and that love conquers all, but we've seen so much misuse and misinterpretation of the word love and abuses of its power that we become suspicious of people who openly express their love for others. In my own quest for acceptable expressions of love I've found the work of Dr. Leo Buscaglia most helpful. He's affectionately called the "Love Doctor" who believes people must hug one another. "Hugs" for Leo express one's love to another.

Each time that I've spoken to groups large or small, I've experienced fear. I am always aware of the tension in my body—butterflies in my stomach, dryness in my mouth, a tightness in my throat which would change my voice quality and dampness in my palms and on my fingers. In those earliest days, I carried many papers in my hands so that I could read them to the audience. My fingers left wet impressions on the papers, the undeniable mark of my fear.

These fears and their consequences are not unique to speakers and performers. Consider for a moment some areas where your fears grow and think of the prices you pay because of the fear's effect upon you.

Perfect love pushes out fear we are taught. Would we be able to apply this principle to allay our fears and improve our performances? Wally Johnston tells us in his book, <u>Take Charge, A Guide To Feeling Good</u>, that we are responsible for how we feel, that we can change our inner attitudes and in that process feel good about ourselves and the world in which we live.

In every audience people actively demonstrate their involvement with the speaker in a variety of ways. I choose to focus specifically on those who express their love with special kinds of "hugs." Some people nod their heads in affirmation with each point expressed. Some people smile. Some wink. Some show tears. People participate as they stand, or raise their hands, or speak to one another. And with each of these "hugs" people send forth the love needed to push my fears away. Believing that these hugs will push away the fears allows me to relax, feel good in front of a group, and then I can give my very best performance.

The next time you accept an invitation to speak to a large group and you feel your fear growing, look at those people in the crowd who want so much for you to succeed. They'll be sending their love in special ways. Use it to push away your fear.

Just as love pushes away fear, increasing fear will push away love. Young men and women who have continued to fail and to accumulate guilt and questions of their own worth strike fear into the minds and hearts of others. That fear pushes away our love, the love they need to overcome the fear which will lead to the next feeling.

ANGER

Anger in people can be reduced through constructive physical outlets. To run, to strike, to clean, to pound, or to shout helps people to release the tremendous build-up of energy at this level. I'm not just sure where I heard this and I'm careful where I say it, but I've heard that "—the angriest women make the lightest bread." Do you suppose there's any truth to that sexist statement?

Some of our angriest people seem to be extremely destructive which suggests to me that their anger needs to get out of their physical bodies. We need to help these people to find positive outlets.

Each October members from my freshman class would accompany my family and me for a long weekend retreat to our mountain home outside of Laramie, Wyoming. At six o'clock in the evening we drove

145

through the gate and into the yard. I knew there would be just enough daylight left to get everything organized for our short stay.

The sheriff's car pulled slowly into the yard, and the sheriff left the car. He spoke hesitantly, "Do you have someone here named Kevin K. from Minnesota?" Kevin came forward to hear the news that his father had gotten his arm entangled in the working portion of a piece of farm machinery. "Your father is in stable condition at the hospital," came the report and Kevin needed to call right away to check on his father.

Throughout the short time we stayed in Wyoming, Kevin spent time at the woodpile chopping relatively large logs into more useable pieces. You would not have believed the force of those swings. The sound echoed throughout the valley. After long sessions with the axe and the wood, Kevin was able to discuss his feelings of fear and guilt.

LONELINESS

Therapeutic agencies recognize the importance of friends in alleviating the loneliness of clients. Having just one friend can be enough to turn someone around in the funnel, and start that person toward the reduced pressure of success. Occasionally helpers reach through the symbolic wall of the funnel only to discover that the energy which had been building through this whole process bursts outward toward the helper. The energy was not originally targeted for the helper. To know enough to stay with the person through these explosive times will mark you as an effective helper of troubled people.

My second year of teaching brought me face to face with what I believed to be an impossible teaching situation. He was sixteen years old and perfectly comfortable with his twelve year old classmates who visited my room once each day of the week for fifty three minutes of instruction in the use of our language. Very quickly I learned that he couldn't spell his own name. How could anyone succeed in English class without the ability to read or write? Social promotion brought him to seventh grade.

Teachers must reach and teach each child I'd been taught, so I turned for help to a good friend, a kindergarten teacher, and she suggested "—show and tell. He has always enjoyed talking and sharing. I scoffed in disbelief, but since no other solution seemed available or workable I chose to give her suggestion a try.

Each Friday I presented a test to all seventh graders over the work covered in the week just now ending. The time existing between the end of the test and the end of the period would be a perfect time for "Seventh Grade Show and Tell." I imposed one rule: "No one could present for a second time until everyone has presented at least once." This would prevent the more capable and extroverted students from monopolizing the stage and would force the less capable and most reluctant kids to take their turns.

Late in the marking period, he came to me, frightened, eyes cast toward the floor, stuttering uncontrollably and saying, "M-m-m-mr. Kern, c-c-could I tell s-s-something, even if I d-d-don't have s-s-something to s-s-show?" He was relieved to see in my face enthusiastic assurance that his telling would be acceptable.

The last hour of the day came and he stood to address the class on his chosen topic, milking a cow by hand. When he mentioned the use of a one-legged stool, the less rural population in the class laughed and provoked him as they guessed he might lose his balance and fall off the stool into unpleasant conditions. He quickly explained that his two feet were on the floor along with the one leg of the stool and that by pushing his head into the cow, he'd easily avoid falling. Nonbelievers were not convinced, so he told us he'd bring a stool to class.

With the confidence which grows from knowing and with defiance toward the doubters in the class, he proudly held his not-too-clean stool high on Monday afternoon and then demonstrated its practicality. I suspected he might resort to more physical behavior had the teasing continued.

Through the remainder of the year, he told of the tail of the cow and its effect on the milker, of training a dog to get the cows, of the cows walking into the same stanchions time after time, and finally of placing a new cow with an established herd. He had succeeded in his language arts activity.

Imagine my surprise when he came in that last week of the year requesting that he receive an "F" in English. I explained that since he had given all those speeches, I'd thought of giving him a "D". "Well," he stuttered, "I'm failing everything else and I'd really like to be in your English class next year." He seemed to realize that there would be an entirely new group moving into seventh grade as the current bunch went on to eighth grade, and that they won't have heard his stories yet.

He was much more confident that second year as he shared many of the same stories. Once again at the end of the year he requested a failing grade. He totally ignored my explanation of the school policy which made it impossible to fail someone a second time, and pleading his own case, he stated, "If you fail me I'm coming back to school next year until my birthday in December. If you don't I'm going to quit right now."

When he returned for his third trip through seventh grade English, he asked that he be excluded from the rule, a rule which was designed to force him to speak. After all he reasoned, "I'm only going to be here until December, and I have all these stories to tell."

Many speeches were delivered during that fall term and in December he turned in his school books. He married in January and thereafter our paths separated.

Recently we met on the streets of a southeastern Minnesota town and he asked if I'd join him in a local tavern for a glass of beer. Not much in the beer tavern was clean and the lights were low. The reminiscing was warm, light and joyous. He stuttered just a bit and his tone changed ever so slightly as he spoke these words, "You know, Mr. Kern, when I was in seventh grade, those three years, I had only one friend, and it was you."

I felt the tears and the choking sensation in my throat as I remembered those early teaching days— low, low salary and much happiness. Today he's an American farmer and if the signs in the farm belt are accurate, he feeds "75 people and You." I'm so pleased he was able to work back through that failure funnel.

<u>Pathway # 4</u>

UNEQUAL RELATIONSHIPS.

Whenever people live in relationships where one person feels inferior to the other, both people will begin to accumulate pain. Whenever we live in realtionships where both persons have equal power, the relationships grow, flourish, and are mutually beneficial. Having said that let's examine what this might mean to you.

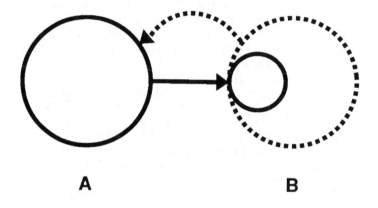

A   **B**

The large solid circle (A) represents the personal power or psychological influence of one person in a relationship. The small solid circle (B) depicts the same for the other. In most interactions Person A will emerge as a winner over Person B. The arrow from A to B symbolizes a flow of information or influence from Person A to Person B, who then chooses resentment to fill the smaller circle to the same size as the larger (broken circle around B). This resentment will be sent to Person A (broken arrow from B to A) and the relationship will be filled with pain. Person A hurts when the resentment hits, and just as acid ruins the vessel in which it is contained, the resentment will destroy Person B.

Working with people in large groups gives me a chance to demonstrate the theory with practical and visual applications. Imagine this. I'm nearly six feet three inches tall and weigh over two hundred pounds. For this demonstration I might choose a very small woman. After introducing her, I would point out that because I was so much larger, I would very likely win most physical contests and my littler partner would lose. I would suggest that losers will get even (resentment flowing), and that losers often seem to have long memories.

The dynamics which operate in physical interaction function much the same way in psychological relationships. In conversation with my partner I would lead her into discovering that we share information with those we perceive as equals, we share little or nothing or sometimes even gossip about others (more resentment) when we believe we're not equals. I would share my observation that sometimes married people tell everyone else what they dislike in each other and play a vicious game in the process—"I'll hold you responsible for what you don't know, and I won't tell you."

Finally I would ask people to consider a married couple or any two people in a relationship:

1. If they love one another, they will share information one with the other (interacting as equals).

2. If they feel nothing for one another they probably will have no interaction—they'll say nothing.

3. If they dislike one another, they will gossip, they will tear one another down each to their own friends, and soon they will destroy the relationship and likely each other.

Think of this homely and practical application. I have a beard and sometimes I accidentally drop food into it. Those who care for me and regard me as equal will tell me it's there so I can brush it away. Those who have no interest in a relationship with me may notice the food and say nothing, but those who see this as a chance to be resentful, will tell someone else, "See old Kern, he's got garbage in his beard again." They may hold me responsible for something I don't know.

> FRIENDS TELL US OF THINGS WE DON'T KNOW.
> HE TOLD ME I'D DROPPED FOOD IN MY BEARD.
> HE IS MY FRIEND.

School administrators gathered in central Wisconsin for a workshop designed to improve the quality of comunication in the workplace. To encourage healthy feedback in relationships, I had spent quite a long time in the early part of the session presenting and reviewing the nature of people able to provide feedback and how people's perceptions of the balance of power would influence the flow of information back and forth.

I'd gone over the lesson several times and wanted to give it one more shot before our morning coffee break. We live with three kinds of people:

1) SOME PEOPLE CARE FOR US: they share with us those things outside our awareness which might be helpful to us.

2) SOME ARE INDIFFERENT IN THEIR FEELINGS: they share nothing at all.

3) SOME PEOPLE DISLIKE US: they tell others what they might have told us. They often hold us responsible for those things we don't know. They gossip.

For a homely example, I described the situation you've heard where I spilled food into my beard and examined relationships based upon the feedback I had received from others.

Approximately one hundred-twenty school administrators had sat for ninety minutes and were quite ready for the morning coffee break. As I reiterated above principles this last time, a school superintendent in the back of the room stood and spoke with his eyes dancing with mischief,"I came into school one morning and walked all through the building for more than two full hours with my fly unzipped. No one told me. Does that mean they don't love me?" Participants burst into laughter.

His principal rose from his chair and stood right beside him. He spoke right out, "No, it means no one was threatened."

Everyone enjoyed the morning break.

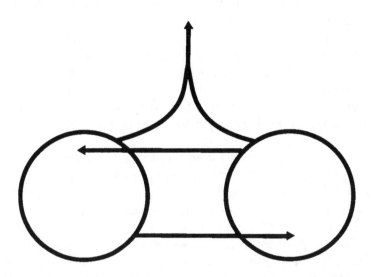

In healthy relationships we work together as equals as much as is possible recognizing the vast differences which exist amongst us. In the most essential areas, being human and being important, I can interact as your equal whoever you are. Each of us grows in this equal interaction. I can share with you those things which may be helpful to you, and you'll share with me from your perspective. Out of this sharing will flow decisions acceptable to each of us. We will not need to store any resentment.

As equals I offer you the benefit of what I see, hear, smell, or know through feedback and I also take the benefits of your senses. As equals we will resolve conflicts as each of us shares our position and we arrive at a solution with which we're both comfortable. As equals we learn to trust one another to be available without being dependent, to be loving without being solicitous, and to be honest without being brutal. As equals we can establish a foundation for a lasting relationship.

In many families parents assume the Big Circle role as they force children into the Small Circle. Over time an enormous problem can develop. Parents who make all major decisions for their children when they're one, when they're five, when they're eight, and when they're eleven will entrust them with the family car and accompanying freedom when they're seventeen. Think of the many ways adolescents find to demonstrate resentment toward parents.

Husbands and wives who treat their spouses as inferior may be angry or hurt when each spends more of his or her time with people who treat them with respect and dignity. In marriages with equality in the partnership, infinite happiness exists.

Administrators in all lines of work acknowledge the value of receiving feedback especially from those employees who are nearest the work. At times subordinates will assume a Small Circle role for themselves, assign a Big Circle role to the boss or supervisor and use this perceived inequality as a justification for gossiping. We become all too familiar with the coffee lounge conversation which centers on the nasty statements made about those in charge. No one wins in these situations; everyone loses. Sharing information with the appropriate person about the things that need improvement will improve our work relationships considerably.

Friends will share information with friends regardless of differences in education, age, race, religion, economic situation, or a number of other variables. I know

how lucky I am when I near the end of a chapter on pain
and my mind is filled with the large number of friends
who have cared enough to share insights and information with me.

James was seventy-nine years old, a wonderful
story teller, and hard of hearing when he appeared at
the first of my scheduled two-day workshops in the
department. When I inquired about his continuing to
work in a department with a mandatory retirement, he
winked, smiled, and spoke loudly, "I lie!"

"When you care for someone you'll tell that person
what he or she needs to know, when you have no
feelings toward another you'll say nothing at all, and
when you dislike someone you'll find yourself telling to
others what you might have told to the one person who
could make a change." Yesterday, I'd spoken these
words, illustrated them, and repeated them again and
again. Today, I wore a T-shirt under my dress shirt
with a hole between the neck band and the body of the
shirt, and as you might have guessed the hole was
directly in the front clearly visible to anyone in front of
me. If they care for me, based on yesterday's lesson,
they'll tell me what they can see that I can't see.

His volume was a bit of a surprise as James came
toward me saying, "Professor Kern, do you know you
have a hole in your T-shirt?" I told him that I knew and
he responded, "I thought so!" Observers in the workshop loved every moment of it.

Our conversation during breaks that day centered
on my home in the Rocky Mountains. James had never
been west of Rapid City and he thought that he and his
wife might come to visit in the summer months. How
lucky I am, I thought, that I'll be able to learn from his
experiences through four decades.

The second of our two-day sessions began on a cold
snowy day four weeks after the first workshop. James
was not present as we began and I worried. Twenty
minutes into my first lecture he appeared at the door in
the back of the room and, having been recognized,
spoke deliberately and loudly, "Professor Kern, I'm
sorry for my tardiness. I've brought a note from my
wife, Mary, explaining why I wasn't here at the beginning." After the anticipated response from the group,
James continued, "My battery was dead." Following a

well timed pause he clarified, "On second thought, it was my car's battery."

After our last meeting he explained, he had visited a doctor only to learn that his driving would be restricted and that he wouldn't be allowed to drive to Laramie. "When I told Mary she told me that we should sell that car and buy tickets to Denver. 'Maybe that kid will pick us up there,' she said. Would you pick us up in Denver?"

My answer demonstrated my excitement at the reality of his coming, "James, I'd pick you up in Los Angeles."

"Well," he drawled, "that won't be necessary; you see, we'll be flying to Denver."

He was missing again on the first day of our third meeting. He'll come, I thought, late as before, to get that center of attention position he enjoyed so much. But the morning ended; he'd not appeared as I knew he would; and I learned of his unexpected and sudden death over lunch with other participants. My first thoughts were selfish and angry—he won't be coming to the mountains—his experiences will not be shared.

In truth, he's very much with me every moment

now as he was with me during that summer of his expected visit to the Rockies. Despite our many differences James demonstrated that he cared by providing me a set of eyes outside my body.

I'm a bit embarrassed to admit that there have been many times when I could have told others things but chose not to share.

On a warm Saturday in August, we would work together to remove the nine upstairs screens and the eleven downstairs screens so that the heavy storm windows could be hung in preparation for the harsh Minnesota winter. In 1950 I was fourteen and she had already passed her seventy-fifth birthday, however, the respect and love we'd learned for one another helped us to bridge age differences.

We were to start early, and as I rang the doorbell my mind was full of anticipation. We would work very hard, the day would be long, and I'd be paid whatever I told her that I had earned. Four rings on the doorbell yielded no response from inside. Is something wrong? I knocked loudly believing the bell wasn't functioning; no one came. I turned to descend the steps and she appeared clothed in her robe and nighty scarf. She laughed heartily as she told of shutting off the alarm and falling asleep.

The preparations for the day's work were completed, she'd gotten herself ready, clothes changed, hair combed, and make-up applied. The rouge she'd applied to her right cheek was considerably higher than the application on her left cheek. Looking directly at me she asked, "How do I look, Jim?"

Her request to take advantage of fourteen year old eyes to supplement her failing eyesight escaped me completely as I assured her that she looked fine. She did not look fine at all.

We shared many laughs that day. She sang, she danced, she pulled the shade down from inside as I washed windows on the outside, and she teased. During our lunch she responded to the doorbell and paid two of my friends, her paperboys, who delivered news to her step each morning. As she spoke with them she knew that she looked fine.

157

At the end of the day she thanked me, she complimented me on a job well done, and she paid me handsomely.

In school on Monday morning, the paperboys laughed maliciously as they poked fun of her appearance. My anger grew with my embarrassment. Had I told her the truth, she could have made the necessary change in her rouge and might not have become the object of such ridicule. I cared for her; I could have told her the truth.

Part IV

Pathways to Joy

BUILD THE FORT...TODAY!

In the two previous sections I have suggested that four essential needs must be satisfied before we know joy in our lives. Let's review them to set the stage for examining five ways for people to increase their joy. People need food, clothing, and shelter to keep their physical bodies healthy. People need love and in receiving love they give it as well. People need to believe they are important, and as we become aware of our own importance, we see the worth of others through the filters of our feelings about ourselves. People need to feel safe and secure, free from psychological abuse as well as physical abuse.

We're all aware of people who seem to have all four of these needs met and still remain joyless and miserable. I believe one more element must be present for people to be filled with joy. We need to know that attaining a joyous position in life requires hard work and continuous attention to the process. Many people including song writers, poets, and philosophers would have us believe different things about getting joy in our lives. Some believe when we're free from pain we're filled with joy. Some believe that when your needs are met, joy will come like a butterfly and light on your shoulder. Some believe that we'll know joy as long as we put our own needs aside and give ourselves completely to others. Some believe we must eat, drink, and make merry, for tomorrow we may die. Some believe that true joy will never exist for us here, that we must endure our stay here in hopes of joy later. Some seem to believe that to be joyous we must live in poverty, and some seem to believe the opposite of that.

I believe that filling your own life with joy is a difficult and lifelong process. I have compared the process to
rowing a boat upstream. Have you done that so you
know what it's like?

My father took me often to the Mississippi River to
fish with him. Before he believed that a motor could be
used efficiently to get the boat to the fish, we'd row the
boat just as he'd done in the "good old days" of his childhood. We'd fished near the shore between the wing dams
built on the river in an attempt to control the water flow.
When it came time to move above one of the dams, we'd
pull on those oars, swing the boat around the end of the
dam into the rapidly flowing water, and, hopefully, slip
right into the quieter area above the dam. If I were to
stop pulling in the area of rapid flow for a even a short
rest, I quickly discovered that the boat did not stay in
the same place. Many people today are flowing with the
current and they wonder why they're eventually dashed
against the rocks or washed up onto the shore. Filling
your life with joy requires constant attention and you
must keep pulling on the oars.

Let me add one footnote to the analogy. When my
dad pulled on the oars, the boat moved easily and went
directly to the chosen spot. When I was "manning" (I
only hoped that's what it was then) the oars, our boat
went to the right and to the left, back and forth, and
frequently I'd stop pulling. Dad patiently encouraged me
to keep working. I suspect my dad had lots of information which I lacked.

I believe I have some information which will help you
to experience joy, that feeling of contentment and happiness which has lasting value. I believe each one of us
must take the responsibility for filling our lives with
those qualities which lead us toward fulfillment and
integrity and away from despair. If something which
follows appears to be helpful to you, grab it and incorporate it into your life.

Pathway # 1

TAKE CHARGE OF YOUR LIFE.

How many times have you heard people say things like these: "My husband said I should....", or "My wife said I had to ...", or "My boss just expects me to ...", or "The law says....", or "The devil made me do it."

Whenever you allow someone else to decide what you'll do with your life you're passing up an opportunity to move toward joy. You have been entrusted with a life to live, take charge of that life and live it.

Little children come into the world with a built in program to run their own lives. They come to us an egocentric, selfish bundle of noise and energy, and we want to help them to live successfully with others in society. In her wonderful books on raising children, Judith Martin admonishes us to civilize these little ones. I sincerely and enthusiastically support what she says and would plead with parents to use care that they don't imprison children in the pain of unreasonable servitude. Children will experience the joy of taking charge if we encourage them to make choices and decisions appropriate to their age level.

In their pre-school years children would like to participate in many activities just beyond their capability. As parents we are responsible for our children's physical safety so we'll hopefully stop any activity where the child might be severely injured. Children are, however, capable of making many of their own decisions, of taking much responsibility for their lives. Children need to have the consequences of their choices come to them. My homely rule of thumb for determining appropriateness goes like this, "I want them to stub their toes without breaking their legs."

A set of guidelines that I've found very helpful to young parents in establishing appropriate behaviors for children comes to our home in a pamphlet entitled the

"Growing Child". (Order it from: 22 N. Second Street, Lafayette, IN 47902)

Taking charge of your life demands that you choose what you'll do or avoid what you don't want to do. Taking charge also suggests that you choose how people will influence you. So many times we let statements or behaviors of other people determine how we feel, how we act, and eventually what kind of person we are. If you could choose to return kindness for unkindness or to turn the other cheek, you will have demonstrated the ability to live your own life, to walk your own path. You probably won't be dashed against the rocks on the shore, and should you find yourself being hurt, you'll make another decision which brings you into the light of joy once more.

Four hundred fourth, fifth and sixth graders came into the room in their typical style and sat on the floor in front of me. "Raise your hands high if someone has said something which has hurt your feelings." Nearly all of them lifted their hands into the air and I continued, "Now raise your hands even higher if anyone has done something which hurt your feelings." As the learners begin to realize that this will be important for them and relevant to their lives, the enthusiasm grows. "Should we work on that a bit this morning before we get into the lesson?" The energy and enthusiasm of this age group filled the room. Even the adults present began to catch the spirit.

I explained that I would say some words and that they should repeat exactly what I said to them. "Are you ready?" I asked, and several of them giggled as they repeated "Are you ready?" They seemed so pleased that they could tease without fear of being reprimanded or embarrassed.

"No matter what you say to me..." The kids' response lacked the drive and conviction I'd expected, so I suggested we try it again only this time with more intensity and I added a gesture, to point directly at me as they spoke to me. "No matter what you say to me..." This time the room rocked. We continued, "...no matter

164

what you do to me..." and the kids spoke right out. "On this last part," I encouraged, "you'll point at yourself as you speak...I'm still an important person." They smiled. Now we want to put it all together, and I cautioned them to watch for the combination. "No matter what you say or do to me, I'm still an important person." We said it fast, we said it slowly, we said it quietly, we shouted it out, and then I asked, "Do you believe what you've been saying?"

We talked together about some of the things others say or do to them and how they don't need to be hurt and sad. Very few of them knew who Eleanor Roosevelt was, but I explained that she taught the world a lovely way to handle this kind of thing when she said, "—they can only hurt you if you give them permission."

I've used the same exercise with adults and afterward I often choose an adult and deliberately say something potentially hurtful directly to them to see if they'll have learned from the lesson. During a session for senior citizens I chose a little woman with glasses in the front row, and said, "Four eyes!"

Imagine my surprise when she returned with, "Stick it in your ear."

Adults, of course, profit by learning this same lesson as many have not learned it earlier in their lives. With adults I follow this lesson with a re-statement of the same thought using different words. Many of the events of our lives are out of our control, but we can always control our responses to those events. We can choose our responses in order that we may live as actors or we can become reactors to the events and in the process remain powerless, helpless and frequently hurt. We can believe that we are not very important persons.

WE CAN'T CONTROL EVENTS—WE CAN
CONTROL OUR RESPONSES.

Remember the last time you drove a car or rode in a car down a rain-soaked roadway? Can you picture a car flashing past and splashing muddy water on your windshield? What thoughts and feelings coursed through your mind as the wiper was activated only to compound the problem?

If you allowed yourself any negative thoughts or feelings, you'll be re-acting. You'll have the upset (to share with others near you perhaps). You'll get the ulcer or tumor or cyst. And imagine for just a moment what effect you'll have on the driver who continues down the road. The other may not even be aware that you have a problem.

As an alternative to the anger, hurt, and disease, take charge of your life and consider a response like this: "There are many things in life more important than muddy water on my windshield." Having chosen this position you're free to keep the dirty windshield in its proper perspective.

What are the events then which are more important and more serious than your dirty windshield? Do several events come flooding into your awareness?

Following a speech to sixth grade kids, Norma came forward to share that the removal of her malignant brain tumor left her with four months to live. She also shared that school was so much fun that she would like to be able to come to school on Saturday and Sunday as well. You see, muddy water on your windshield doesn't matter much compared to this.

In my next meeting with the lower elementary I met Billy, a five year old with spina bifida, who, after describing his condition, said, "Don't worry Mr. Kern, they're doing a lot of research now, and who knows—?" I watched him run off and concluded that from now on I would get ulcers and sickness only for something quite important if at all. We can control our responses when we can't control the events!

Take Charge of your life today. Take Charge of your life so you can avoid being misused or abused. Take Charge of your life so that you will never burn out. Take Charge of your life so that you can improve the quality of that life by making the changes you want to make. Take Charge of your life so that when all about you changes, you'll survive on your own. Take Charge of your life so that you can choose your own joy. It's your life, Take Charge of it and Live.

Pathway #2

SELF WORTH

You've heard or read the beautiful line which speaks directly to your worth, "God made you, and God don't make junk", still many of us carry messages about ourselves from childhood to old age which contradict that thought. Some of the junk in our lives might be those messages, so let's be aware of them now, take charge of our lives and discard the junk to its proper place, the junk pile. We've been compared unfavorably to others, we've been labeled, we've allowed words from people to hurt us deeply, and we've been taught to be humble, contrite, self-effacing, and modest. Sometimes we've been treated as dirt under the feet of others. We've experienced guilt, judgment, and ridicule. At those times when we've been hurt by significant people, the trip back to prizing and cherishing ourselves can seem as long as the trip home for a young baseball player. He knew he was worthwhile and he'll know that again one day.

Imagine his pride and joy when he learned he

would be the only player from his small town chosen to participate in the Little League All Star Game to be played in mid-August at the state capital. Many congratulations and encouraging statements motivated him to strive to represent his area well. Two favorite people, his uncle and a family friend, would ride along to watch the all stars participate.

He disguised his disappointment pretty well when he learned that he wouldn't start the game. His spirit, his chatter, and his encouragement of unfamiliar teammates would show the coach that he was ready. From his position right beside the coach on the bench, he leaped up at every chance to cheer his team onward.

In the last of the fifth inning, with his team trailing eight to nothing, he moved a bit down the bench away from the coach. There would be only two more innings. Couldn't the coach sense his desire? Couldn't he go into the game, even if only for a short time? How could he

show his skills without a nod from the coach? This is an All Star game. Couldn't all of the chosen stars have a chance to participate? No one needs to return home having not played.

He'd taken the seat on the bench farthest from the coach as his team batted in the top of the last inning.

His glove was on the ground in front of him now. He didn't leave the bench at all when the lead-off batter hit his single. A ground ball to the pitcher and two strike outs later, and the all star game was history.

He threw his glove into the trunk of the car in preparation for the long ride home. He probably heard the statements in the car from those who loved him and were proud of him: "You know, it's quite an honor to have been selected as an All Star." "Many players weren't chosen." "We'll hang the picture of the All Star team in the family room. You're right there in the front row." "We were all so proud of you today."

He must have been sleeping. His eyes were shut for the entire trip home.

How would your life change if you were to spend some time each day considering the "all star" part of you? Think for a moment of your uniqueness. There's no other person just like you. You've been given special gifts to use in any way that you choose. Why not choose to use these gifts in such a way that people notice you? Think for a moment of the people who like you; often those who know you very well, like you. What is it about you that they like? Think of how much your life will change when you begin to like those same things about yourself. As you let others see the gifts you have, they'll like you even more and you'll discover even more reasons to care for yourself.

When you develop this more positive view of yourself, you'll start to request the best and you'll not settle for less. After all precious priceless people deserve the very best. If you find one pathway blocked in your attempt to get the best for yourself, Take Charge and discover another way to go. Never, never give up!!

I'd worked with him before. He was very creative and worked very hard, but his positive, hopeful, and optimistic outlook really impressed me. After I'd learned to know him better I discovered someone who would not settle for less than the best for himself or for the students he served.

He was the principal of a center city elementary school who seemed totally unaffected when only six people appeared at the home-school meeting. We had prepared for one hundred or more. The chairs were all ready, the snacks in place and some of us were obviously disappointed at the low turnout.

He walked before the six, welcomed them, and introduced me to the "crowd". We re-arranged the chairs so we could sit in a circle to talk and to learn. I began by sharing my talk and the discussion began. Four people joined the group in the next ninety minutes and many people raised personal and important questions about being effective parents.

The meeting ended in a very happy way. All ten left with some specific strategies to use in working with their children and I sat with him over a cup of coffee.

When I reflected his comfortable attitude about the low number of people, he told me a story he had remembered from the "character lessons" which were a required part of his early education.

"The boy approached the Master with a request that He teach him, and the Master declined telling the boy that He couldn't teach just one, that there would need to be twenty before he could teach. "The child gathered nineteen dolls, placed them on chairs, took the last chair himself, and said, 'Now, Master, will you teach us? Now there are twenty.' "And the Master taught. And the boy learned."

As we continued to talk he pointed out that he knew that for each of the persons who attended the meeting, there could have been nineteen dolls there also.

Pathway # 3

SELF REGULATION

By self regulation I mean that you can place limits on your own behavior and I'll suggest that by choosing moderation you'll begin to feel better about who you are and you'll experience a deeper joy.

In my mind discipline means the very same thing as self regulation and using this meaning we would know that no one 'disciplines' another. 'Control' more closely describes those forces or techniques delivered from outside a person. So what would this tell parents and all others who want to raise children with self regulation? I believe in telling youngsters, "I will control you until you provide evidence that you can effectively control yourself, and at that point you will have control over your life. Should you then demonstrate that you cannot or will not regulate yourself, I'll once again exercise my responsibility to control you."

Any person who lives a disciplined life reduces many stresses considerably and conserves energy for use on other areas to attain joy.

Another word closely related to self regulation is the word 'moderation.' I'm convinced that experimentation with many different things in our lives provides the excitement, the exhilaration, and the spice which keeps us interesting and alive.

What we do in moderation probably won't harm us very much, but excesses, one consequence of no self regulation, will most certainly be harmful.

I've encouraged many parents to consider the example they provide for their children in the area of self regulation. Here perhaps more than any other area we see the effects of the guiding principle, "Do as I say, not as I do." When we disregard self regulation in ourselves, the example we give children says that discipline isn't very important yet if the children lack discipline (self control) we become enraged at them. Do we smoke excessively? Do some of us eat excessively? Do we drink excessively? Have we driven too fast without getting caught? Have we written checks without having money in the bank? Have we driven after drinking? Do we tell stories with sexual stereotypes or suggestions when children are present?

Having considered those questions let's turn our attention to some of the statements we might hear from adults as they discuss the major problems of today's teenagers. "Our kids just don't have any self control and the schools have no control over them either—They're all using drugs, you know—They drive so recklessly nowadays—Too many girls are sexually active and they're getting pregnant—They don't know how to handle money—The girls are starving themselves to death." Lacking discipline we deprive ourselves of joy and teach our children to live without joy as well.

To learn about discipline and moderation by trying the limits of our abilities implies taking some risks. Risking can be dangerous and can have very negative consequences. I really don't want my children to break their legs as they're stubbing their toes. This taught Paul and Chris about self regulation and may have positive residuals today, but at the time I doubted my philosophy.

Both of my boys wanted to ride that big motorcycle long before their physical bodies had developed enough to make the task safe and easy. While I had no objection to their learning to ride, I didn't want them to be hurt. "The machine has no mind of its own to protect you from danger," I had repeatedly warned.

We agreed that they could learn to ride it as soon as they could straddle the cycle, hold it upright and touch the ground on each side of the bike. Chris was able to demonstrate his ability to do these three things on the last day of a relatively short vacation in the mountains.

"Keep the bike in low gear and ride only inside the fence," I cautioned. He couldn't get enough of the riding; down and back, down and back. I sat on the porch and watched every move. He really rode quite well and I was proud of his accomplishment.

During a rare break in the riding sessions with the cycle shut down and resting, Paul and Chris piled two small mounds of dry earth in such a way that the bike could be pulled between them. I returned to supervise Chris's riding only to find Paul on the bike with his feet planted carefully on the tops of the mounds of dirt. He sat proudly aboard the large cycle and balanced it easily with the assist from the earth piles. His eyes had that hopeful look which seemed to say, "Now I can ride, too." I had promised.

We agreed that Chris would watch as Paul rode and Paul would watch as Chris rode. The motorcycle got no rest at all for the remainder of the afternoon.

Squeezing time and again on the handle grip to manipulate the clutch lever wore a painful and large blister on Paul's small hand at the base of his thumb. In an attempt to ease the pain, Paul rested the heel of his hand on the handle grip without the thumb locked over the bar as a safety measure. Riding the cycle was so important that the pain of a blister would need to be ignored for today.

After dinner both boys pleaded for the opportunity to ride out of the yard, south on the road to the cattle guard and back. Against my better judgment I agreed on one last trip apiece to the cattle guard and back. "Can we shift to second gear?" Both were capable so we agreed second gear would be fast enough.

Chris would go first and we watched as he negotiated each turn and each change with ease. As Paul left the yard he seemed to shift awkwardly. I thought nothing of it as I was unaware of the blister and the unsafe adjustment he had made. The U-turn was completed, he's heading home. Just one more turn through the gate, down the driveway and we can put the bike away.

As he shifted from second gear into first gear, his

clutch hand slipped away and the bike with its rider plunged out of control into the barrow pit. With each bump the tiny hand on the accelerator moved, the speed of the bike was continually increased, and a three-strand barbed wire fence lay straight ahead of him. The top wire was neck high to the boy. My heart stood still and I'm sure Paul's world moved ever so slowly.

Just moments before the bike and rider hit the fence, the front wheel hit a large bump and flew high into the air. The weight and force of the bike broke all three wires and Paul stayed with the bike as it tipped over inside the fence.

He had only one small scratch on his arm but more importantly had an object lesson in regulating himself and his own behavior.

I trust both Paul and Chris on those bikes now as I'm sure they know that even one moment out of control, one moment of inattention, or one moment without discipline could result in tragedy.

Pathway # 4

GIVING AND RECEIVING

We'll know joy in our lives when we learn to give and

to receive and to do each one graciously. I know that I have less trouble giving than receiving and in previous sections I've shared some of the reasons for this.

Giving something, sharing something, has always seemed so—well, so nice, and I wanted significant others to think that I was nice so I learned to give. Receiving on the other hand seemed to make me uncomfortable. Somehow I believed that when I received something I was in debt, I believed that now I would be obliged to "give back" to bring us back to "even". Stretching the thinking to an illogical conclusion, I could never be "even" with all that people had given me.

I'm not sure I was aware at the time, but giving always seemed to be more enjoyable if the receiver got excited and sincerely demonstrated happiness with my gift. I can see it clearly now; as we give, we receive, and as we receive, we give.

This balance between giving and receiving can be easily understood if one thinks for only a moment about a child receiving a gift which had been anticipated for a day or longer. The excitement of the receiving child fills the giver with immeasurable joy. With young children back in my life, I'm abundantly filled with joy whenever I give something to these precious little ones.

Pathway # 5

HAVING FUN

Joy comes to those who realize the importance of having fun. Here I am writing at the end of this section, and I can think of nothing which would give me greater joy than to give each of you permission to Have Fun at least once each day of your life. I meet with people all over the world who spend so much of their time and their energy in their work that there's little of either left to re-create themselves with some fun activity. All work and no play may make us dull, and will certainly increase our stress.

Something I call fun may be an absolute chore for another so I must take charge of my own life and choose something which gives me pleasure. To arrive at joy in your life, you must choose activities which are fun for you. I'm somewhat amused that airlines have chosen to reward frequent flyers with an opportunity to fly off for a "fun filled" trip somewhere. A ride on an airplane is a part of my work and I may not see that as fun. With these frequent flyer bonuses, however, I can bring relatives here to visit us; that's fun.

Many traveling people who are married to stay-at-home spouses experience a unique situation in reaching joy in marriage. Denise looks forward to our next "date" while she works diligently with the child care, my schedule, and homemaking. A fun filled experience for her might include a nice dinner at a restaurant and perhaps a night in a nice motel; all of the things I do in connection with my work! Fun for me would be spending an evening at home with the children, a nice home cooked meal, and a good night's sleep in my own bed; all of which she does when she works! We've worked hard to do things fun for each of us.

One popular values clarification exercise requires people to write quickly "Twenty Things You Love To Do" then you assess your values by examining several variables which stem from your fun list, for example, do you prefer alone activities, expensive or cheap, active or quiet, etc. Participants frequently record the last time they did each of these things. I'm sorry for those people who learn that they aren't doing the things they love to do. I rejoice with those people who have done all twenty things in the past week or less. One student had done all twenty things in the past twenty four hours. Are you doing your "fun" things?

I enjoy building things out of wood (carpenters may not choose this) and working on my cars (auto mechanics may not choose this), but being on the road makes these nearly impossible. My search to find an activity which would allow me to construct something while I was away from home, brought me to try needlecraft.

Because of a prolonged illness during my second grade year in school, I spent a goodly amount of time with my grandmother who taught me to knit and to crochet. While I was in high school classmates knew that I had committed myself to knitting a sweater for a special friend. Later on, having read books on craft work for men (for example: Rosie Greer's well known work in the area, "Men and Needlepoint") and receiving encouragement and tutoring from my wife, Denise, I began to stitch in earnest.

I find needlecraft to be very enjoyable and immensely relaxing. I began working on latch hook rugs, and then when the seats on the planes were moved closer together I moved on to less bulky crafts, needlepoint, and counted cross stitch. I seldom leave home without at least one project.

Many hours of my life are spent on airplanes, in airports, or in motel rooms with very little to do after I've read everything available and have completed my bookwork. I keep my sewing stashed away in my briefcase and as I settle into the aisle seat with two men between me and the window, I'll often shut my eyes and think about the day behind me or the trip ahead. After the plane leaves the ground and getting off is no longer an option for passengers, I bring out my briefcase, remove my sewing and begin to work. I will admit that I have fun watching the reaction of the man beside me.

On one such occasion my seat partner sat quietly and watched me work. He seemed to be rather interested in what I was doing. He spoke to me as the plane was descending into Logan Airport at Boston saying, "Pardon me, are you Roosevelt Greer?" He had noted that we were both "—big and did needlecraft." We both enjoyed a wonderful laugh at the mistaken identity.

In Conclusion

... with many thanks!

BUILD THE FORT...TODAY!

In this short concluding comment I propose to offer you three gifts, my way of giving you something I hope you'll use. As you receive and use these gifts bear in mind that you'll be giving in your receiving. All members of my family learned about the beauty of giving and receiving years ago when we faced another holiday with absolutely no extra money for gifts.

We voted to make homemade gifts this Christmas because with Dad in graduate school, we had no money to buy gifts.

Paul, age seven, made a special gift for his mother. He took a one by six board about fifteen inches long; he nailed a cleat on one end with the only nails he could find, sixteen penny nails. He lay the cleat on our round oak table, he placed the board on top of it, and he drove two nails quite deeply into the table.

I encouraged him not to do that again. He nailed a cleat on the other end of the board, and when he noticed the ends of the nails sticking out, he whacked them over. It was an ugly looking thing. I didn't think it was improved at all after he'd covered it with aluminum foil, but he was satisfied. He wrapped it with Christmas wrap and wrote his message on the outside, "To my mother, with love, your son, Paul."

When she opened her gift on Christmas morning, she did not ask what it was. Instead she asked Paul to tell her a story about it.

He was so very serious as he explained his gift, "Well, Mom, I notice when we have company, we have meat loaf, and you don't have a dish big enough to put it on. Mom, this is a meat loaf holder."

"Well, Paul, we can use it tonight." We did have meat loaf that night, served on the ugliest meat loaf holder you could imagine. The glow gleamed on his face. His gift was being received and was being used.

181

Even now when we have meat loaf, Paul sits at the table knowing that he could build a better meat loaf holder now, but this one was built eighteen years ago by a seven year old boy, and his gift is still being received and used.

If our paths should cross eighteen years from today, I'll be filled with joy that you've received and are using these gifts.

Gift# 1

THE GIFT OF LIFE

I know, I know!! You're saying you already have life. Do you really live or do you exist as so many people do? People who live know that they can laugh and they laugh frequently. People who live know that tears come from time to time and that we don't need to be embarrassed or try to hide those tears. People who live take chances, they know pain, they experience joy, and they make a difference.

When we're least prepared, life gets away. I was in my office when the phone rang. My mother told me that Dad had carried the luggage from their motel room to the car and had complained of dizziness. He lay on the couch and even before she could get an ambulance there he died.

I turned to my friend, Wally, who comforted me. "It really hurts when you lose your dad." I knew that he understood. I cried, I was angry, and Wally suggested that my children have a chance to work through this grief with me. I went home, Chris was there with his back to the sink saying, "Dad, something's wrong."

"Yes, I've just learned that your grandpa died."

"Oh, good, Dad," he said, "now he'll hear all of your speeches."

I remembered the first time he had heard me speak. He sat in the middle of the room. I noticed him covering his mouth several times during my speech, and each time his thumb moved up toward his eyes. At the end of my talk, he placed a strong hand on my arm and shared these words, "Son, I think you'd ought to do that more often."

"Yes, Dad, I love you, too." I think it's the only way he could say it.

GIFT# 2

THE GIFT OF LOVE

That brings me to my second gift, the gift of love. I just don't go to people I don't know and say, "I love you." Instead, I'd like to get to know you. I've invited many people to visit us in our Wyoming home. Should you come, we'll get to know each other. We'll go for a walk together and our love will grow. We'll have a meal together and our love will grow. If you're interested, we'll take a motorcycle ride, and the love will grow.

Then, after we've had a chance to know one another I can tell you I love you.

Gift # 3

THE GIFT OF LAUGHTER

I believe we just don't laugh enough any more. There's not too much funny any more—oh, we have an election every four years, and they seem to get funnier all the time.

I go to prisons, schools, hospitals, and churches, and I find little laughter. Then I visit an old folks home and I find that people laugh frequently and easily. People in the twilight of their lives have learned the therapeutic value of laughter.

After my talk in a senior center, the people (mostly men) line up to tell me their favorite story. Each time I laugh at a story, the line gets longer. The stories have circulated around the home and I'm often the only person there who hasn't heard them. I'm a one person audience.

As a farewell at this point, let me share a story or two told to me by wonderful gentlemen in senior centers.

"An older man and woman sat on the senior center porch and they argued. She challenged him with, "I'll bet I can tell how old you are."

"He came back, "I'll bet you can't," and they carried on like eight year old children, "...bet I can." "...bet you can't."

In exasperation he said, "All right, do it."

"Stand right over there," she directed, "and take off all of your clothes." He did just as she had instructed. After she carefully looked him up and down, she stated confidently, "You're ninety four!"

"How did you know that?" he demanded.

"You told me yesterday."

* * * * * * * * * *

When they put him in the resthome he was unhappy. He didn't know anyone and didn't really want to know anyone here. All the residents gathered in the social hall on his first night there and he looked at them from his place at the door. One woman smiled warmly his direction each time he looked at her. She winked the last time and he walked deliberately toward her demanding to know why she was smiling and winking at him. She spoke rather timidly saying, "You just remind me so much of my third husband."

"How many times have you been married?" His voice expressed his momentary aggravation.

She looked down and spoke quietly, "Two."

* * * * * * * * * *

"I just can't hear anymore," the older man told the doctor during a routine examination.

"Well, let's have a look in those ears." The right ear was clear and the doctor looked into the left ear and was surprised at what he saw there. "Your ear's plugged," he said as he reached for his large tweezers. The object was removed and the doctor held it high enough so each of them could see it. "It surely looks like a suppository to me," the doctor offered.

The older man thought only a moment and laughed as he spoke, "Then I know where my hearing aid is!",

BUILD THE FORT...TODAY!

Jim's Diamond Days

Monday, September 21, 2015

At breakfast Jim asked if I were going to sell the place. I said, "No. I wanted to provide a place for people to stand while they put themselves together." I told him of the dream I had just had. I told Jim I would carry on his work and I would use what he had taught me. Jim told me I needed to help others now. He said I had already done my work. He asked what I would work at full time. I told Jim I wouldn't work full time again. I told him I needed flexibility to help our kids, and their kids, and to continue his work. Jim smiled broadly.

Tuesday, September 22, 2015
Carrie's birthday…

I took Jim to get his Velcade injection. His blood pressure was 60/44. The nurse complained about the inaccuracy of the machine. She took the pressure on his other arm. This time it was 66/45. Dr. G. came down the hall and said the fateful words. "You have to go to the hospital." Jim quietly complied as he stood slowly, walking unsteadily to the door. This was the third hospitalization in three months. What did this mean? Carrie came down and spent the night with Jim in the hospital.

Wednesday, September 23, 2015

Jim was responding to the IV antibiotic. Carrie went back to Austin to work, taking Ollie with her so I could be with Jim. Late evening, I came back out to the house, showered and got clothes and went back to the hospital to spend the night with Jim.

Thursday, September 24, 2015
About 2:00 a.m.

I awoke to a flurry of activity in the room. Jim's heart rate was elevated as was the bilirubin level in his liver. His blood pressure was difficult to stabilize. There were signs of fluid on his lungs and the infection did not seem to be responding to the antibiotics now. Jim and I looked at each other wondering what was next. I crawled into his hospital bed and snuggled up next to him. He held me in his arms as we both drifted off to sleep. We awoke about 7:00 and had some wonderful quiet time together. We talked about life and how we loved each other and how we had no regrets about how we had lived our lives and most of all, how we had no regrets about how we had handled Jim's cancer. I asked him what he wanted to do. He promptly replied, "What do you want to do"? I chuckled and stated, "I asked you first." He looked at me tenderly and said, "I think I have a double sided coin and both sides are coming up tails." We discussed our plan for quality over quantity with no pain, no intubation, and above all a coherent mind. I asked him if he were afraid. He said firmly, "Not at all." We would wait to talk to Dr. G before we decided for sure toward Hospice. I told Jim I would do what he needed me to do. I would follow our plan. Jim said, "Remember the song, I Did It My Way"? I nodded. He said, "I think we should rename it and say, We Did It Our Way". I agreed. As I sat beside Jim, looking into his eyes, I told him I knew where he was going and that he would be waiting for me on the other shore. I stated emphatically, "You have to try to contact me. You have to. I don't know what form that will be or how you will do it, but you have to try to communicate with me." He just listened very intently. Dr. G. came in a little after 1:00 p.m. I asked what exactly we were looking at here. Dr. G. explained that the body can handle two major things going on fairly easily. However, when a third major issue is added it becomes much more challenging. I asked if we were looking at Hospice. He stated maybe, but he wanted to try a powerful antibiotic that can only be given in the ICU. We agreed to do that and see how that went before we made our decision. Shortly thereafter, the ICU Dr. came in to talk with us. As he entered, Jim said quietly to me, "Who's that"? I whispered in his good ear, "I think it's the grim reaper." Jim grinned. The Dr. was an intelligent and experienced professional with a special compassion for those facing life or death. He told us the ICU was full so he would send the nurses down to our private room to administer the IV antibiotic. While they did that, he would review Jim's chart and come back and talk with us. The IV procedure proved to be very painful because the nurse couldn't hit the vein. After several unsuccessful attempts, Katie requested a different nurse come in and insert the IV. Michael, the charge nurse, came in, got Jim all set and then talked with us for awhile. As it turned out he would be Jim's nurse through the night, along with Loretta, an experienced ICU nurse. The Dr. returned about an hour later and asked us if everyone was here that needed to make the decision. We said, "yes" and he began to give us the report. He looked at Jim and I directly explaining there was one more procedure we could try. It was called a central line. The percentage for success was 50-50 and the process was extremely painful for the patient. I kept my promise to Jim and stated we did not want to do that procedure. We would opt to enter Hospice. Jim would be taken home in the morning. Carrie and Katie were already in the room. Josh came back from the airport with Jamie in tow. Thomas stopped by. And the storytelling began. Jim shared the most; one funny story after another. It was a wonderful evening.

Friday, September 25, 2015
8:00 a.m.

The social worker came in to arrange the ambulance home. I explained we were members of the Bulverde/Spring Branch EMS Link. This meant the ambulance would pick us up and take us home for whatever cost our insurance would pay. The social worker discovered the Link does not transport from the hospital back home, only from home to the hospital. Not five minutes later, BSB EMS had called back and said, "Yes, they would pick Jim up and take him home." (I knew Judy had something to do with this!) Jordan, the chief, and David, the mechanic, arrived to collect us. They had arranged a very special ride for Jim and I. I got to ride in the back beside Jim. David drove and Jordan kept us company for the forty-minute ride. We had the windows uncovered so we could see the lovely countryside and sunshine as we drove. It was a beautiful day. Carrie had picked Chris up at the airport and arrived shortly after the ambulance. Paul was on his way and would arrive this evening. Jim sat in his Aggie chair and rested. Theo, Gamze, Saiah and Khias visited briefly. Jim moved to the downstairs bedroom after their visit. I sat with Jim after we got him settled. I asked how he felt. He said, "Comfortable." Jim looked at me with the tenderness he saved for our private moments. He said quietly, "You are beautiful." I smiled as I thanked him. He then said, "It's a beautiful day." I nodded, "Yes, it's a beautiful day." Jim lay back to rest. We made sure someone was with him all the time.

6:30 p.m.

Paul arrived

6:45 p.m.

Jim called me to the bedroom. We heard thunder. It was a welcome sound as it signaled the abatement of a severe drought in our area. The rain began to fall softly at first, then developed into a downpour; drenching the ground for the next two hours. Jim and I chatted. Then he told me he wanted to talk with each child one at a time. Jim asked for each specifically; Paul first, then Chris, then Jamie, then Josh. Katie came into the room with Josh. Jim asked Josh if it's okay if Katie is in there too. Josh responded, "I'm pretty sure it's okay if she's in here too." Then came Carrie's turn. Then I went back in. Jim asked for everyone to come back in. We all encircled the bed and Josh said a blessing. Katie helped me prepare the bed so Jim would be comfortable and I could sleep beside him.

Saturday, September 26, 2015
4:00 a.m.

Jim awoke, needing to go the bathroom. He was a bit confused and noticeably weaker.

4:30 a.m.

I had to wake Jamie to help Jim this time. I was not strong enough to help him now... Jim continued to fade today; sleeping deeply most of the day. The nurse suctioned his lungs to help his breathing. Pastor Dave Galbraith came out for a visit. He checked on all family members. Dave and I walked down the walking path. Dave said at the end of our walk, "This place would make a fabulous retreat center." I said, "Interestingly enough, Jim and I were just talking about what to do and I want to provide a place for people to stand while they put themselves together." Jim had been sleeping all day. He opened his eyes once when Carrie told him "Pam says good-bye". Pastor Dave had a meaningful prayer as we all gathered around the bed. Pastor Dave left. We had goulash and Dr. Pepper as we sat around Jim's bed. We sat the laptop up so we could watch the Aggie game. The Aggies were struggling badly. Josh said, "Dad, you've got to do something! The Aggies are losing!" We watched as the Aggies rallied and ended up winning the game against Arkansas. We sat around telling individual stories about Jim with each one of us. The nurse left.

9:45 p.m.

As I was sitting at Jim's side trying to decide what to do next, Jim suddenly awoke. His eyes were wide with excitement. His countenance was one of pure ecstasy. He looked directly at me and asked in rapid succession, "Denise, is it really you? Is it really you? Is it really you?" I was holding him tightly saying, "Yes, its really me!" Jim uttered a little giggle, stating in a laughing tone, "I can't believe I'm here!" Jim looked around the room, calling out the names of each one there; Chris, Carrie, Paul, Katie, Josh, Jamie. He exclaimed each time with the same query, "Joshua, is it really you?" "Jamie is it really you?" Then Jim asked a question of each that only they would know to what he was referring. He was verifying the reality of him being back with us. Then Jim looked again at me and said, "Jesus told me I could come back and talk to you. I have been with him." Jim asked for help sitting up. We helped him drape his legs over the edge. Jim asked Josh to say the prayer he said Friday night again. As we all bowed our heads Josh eloquently prayed again. Our hearts were so full. The blessings were flowing. Jim began stating emphatically, "First Timothy 1, 2." I repeated the phrase back to him. "First Timothy 1,2." He stated it again, making sure I understood. "First Timothy 1,2". I repeated it again, "First Timothy 1,2". Jim was insistent. "First Timothy 1,2." I held his face in my hands. I looked directly into his joyful eyes and said firmly, "I've got it. First Timothy 1,2." Then as I held his face close to mine, our foreheads almost touching, our eyes locked in our own private communication. I declared so all could hear me, "I promise I will never again doubt or argue with God. I know you have been with him and you are preparing a place for us." I felt Jim's hands on the back of my head. He pulled my face close and kissed me deeply, passionately, and hard with an intimacy we experienced often, just never with our children watching. Jim said, "I love you" and pulled back far enough so he could look me in the eyes again and said, "And the two shall become one." I smiled and said through my tears, "And the two shall become one." He grinned and said, "Only you would know that." I responded, "Yes, only I would know that." Jim continued to talk to each one, saying special things that were uniquely theirs together. He asked about the Aggie game and who had won. He thought we were playing Alabama. Jamie told him, "no" it was Arkansas and the Aggies had won. Jim stood up four separate times. He marched and said, "see, I'm doing my exercises"; the ones the therapist had taught him on Thursday morning. Jim asked for water. Carrie brought him a drink. He had a sip and said, "that's too warm. Bring me cold water. "Jim also took a sip of the Boost energy drink Carrie had brought. As he sat back down on the bed for the last time Jim began to pray the Lord's prayer. We all joined him at the second line, saying the prayer in unison. Jim said he needed to lie down again. He was getting tired. As he lay back he called each of us by name again, gazing at each of us. He asked for M-o-l-l-y, deliberately stressing the sounds. Then he asked for O-l-l-i-e; even requesting Ollie be placed beside him on the bed. As Ollie jumped down, Jim lay back and closed his eyes. I stroked his forehead gently for a short while. Then I leaned over him and said quietly in his ear, "Go with God." And he drifted into a deep sleep. I took a shower and prepared for bed. Katie had made the bed sideways so I could sleep beside him as they pushed the hospital bed up next to the end of the bed. I remember thinking Jim's breathing was so loud that I wouldn't be able to sleep. But it was a regular rhythm, and I quickly drifted off...

Sunday, September 27, 2015
2:25 a.m.

I awoke suddenly to a totally quiet room. Jim was gone. I reached over and touched him. His forehead was cold. I knew he had left a while before. I went out to tell the others. Josh was coming down the stairs with Thea. She had been awake for about forty-five minutes; chatting and carrying on, refusing to sleep. We called the nurse and he called Julio. Both came over. Julio checked Jim's vitals and pronounced him dead at about 4:00 a.m. But Jim had been gone long before then. Julio called Doeppenschmidts'; the funeral

home. The nurse and Julio left. Everyone went to sleep while
I rocked Thea and waited for the hearse to arrive. As I saw
the lights come down the driveway, I opened the front door.
Ollie came to join me in the doorway. I stood holding Thea
waiting for the two men to walk up the sidewalk with the
stretcher. Ollie sniffed their shoes but never made a sound.
Mark introduced himself as well as his helper, Andrew. Both
were good sized men, capable of handling a large body.
Since the stretcher would not make the corner into the room,
Mark and Andrew wrapped Jim gently in the sheet. Mark
said he hadn't realized Jim was so tall. I encouraged them
to take the old blanket as well. Mark was glad so they could
fully wrap him, including his feet, since the sheet was too
short. The two men carried Jim carefully, gently resting him
in the hallway, as they changed their grip and lifted again.
As they lay him on the stretcher both lost their balance
and nearly landed on top of Jim. I stated, "That's the true
definition of dead weight." The two men chuckled softly and
raised the stretcher. They draped a wine colored velvet cover
over Jim. The cover was so regal, it reminded me of royalty.
I said as much, ending with, "Jim always said, when I'm
King this will (or won't) happen... So now you are dealing
with King James." Ollie followed the stretcher all the way to
the hearse. I had gone part way down the sidewalk with Thea
sleeping soundly in my arms. As the men loaded Jim into the
black vehicle, Ollie turned and came back to stand beside
me. We watched the hearse drive slowly and silently out of
sight. I noticed the stark brilliance of the full moon. It was a
moon like the one on the eve of my father's death. I would
learn later there had been a spectacular lunar eclipse during
the time Jim was with us. He had talked with us for an hour
and one half. He had kept his promise. He had contacted
me. We had just witnessed a miracle. Jim had indeed been
sitting at the right hand of God. He had seen Jesus. Jesus
had given him permission to come back and talk with us. .
Jim had shared the last supper with us, he had prayed the
Lord's Prayer with us. He had assured we all knew he was

alive in heaven. Who could deny him that kind of joy? Jim exemplified the phrase, "A Life Well Lived." He continued to teach us throughout his last hours. He continues his lessons even now... I feel him with me most of the time. I see him in the sunrise. I see him in the moonlight. I talk to him as I always have. He continues to share his ideas with me; they appear without warning especially after I have asked for help.

I miss his physical presence.
I miss the twinkle in his eye.
I miss the smile on his lips.
I miss the way he says things.
I miss his arms around me.
I miss his hands.
I miss his bald head.
I miss his voice.
I miss his mischievousness.
I miss his sense of humor.
I miss the feel of his body next to me as I curl up to sleep.
I miss his smell...

How lucky I am to have loved so deeply.
How thankful I am to miss him so completely.
I love you Jim, now and forever. Thank you for being my husband.
Denise